Good Counsel

Good Counsel

A Walking Dialogue with William James

Matt J. Rossano

ROWMAN & LITTLEFIELD
Lanham • Boulder • New York • London

Published by Rowman & Littlefield
An imprint of The Rowman & Littlefield Publishing Group, Inc.
4501 Forbes Boulevard, Suite 200, Lanham, Maryland 20706
www.rowman.com

86-90 Paul Street, London EC2A 4NE

British Library Cataloguing in Publication Information available

Library of Congress Cataloging-in-Publication Data

Names: Rossano, Matthew J., author.
Title: Good counsel : a walking dialogue with William James / Matt J. Rossano.
Description: Lanham : Rowman & Littlefield, [2024] | Includes bibliographical references and index.
Identifiers: LCCN 2024016341 (print) | LCCN 2024016342 (ebook) | ISBN 9781538191996
    (cloth) | ISBN 9781538192009 (paperback) | ISBN 9781538192016 (epub)
Subjects: LCSH: James, William, 1842-1910. | Philosophy. | Psychology. Classification: LCC B945.
    J24 R66 2024 (print) | LCC B945.J24 (ebook) | DDC 191—dc23/eng/20240603
LC record available at https://lccn.loc.gov/2024016341
LC ebook record available at https://lccn.loc.gov/2024016342

Contents

Introduction

The Problem

William James is arguably America's most important intellectual. While the typical university psychology student learns his name, what is learned beyond that is paltry: He wrote a highly influential psychology textbook. He developed a counterintuitive theory of emotion. He was part of the Functionalist School of Psychology. His brother was Henry James, the famous novelist. The subset of students who take a history of psychology class gets more. However, even this is usually restricted to his psychological writings on topics such as the stream of thought, emotion, attention, habits, and personality. This is disappointing, if not shameful, for a man who, in the estimation of Alfred North Whitehead, was as important to the Western intellectual tradition as Plato, Aristotle, and Leibniz.

This sad state, however, is understandable. Jamesian scholarship has become another specialized subdiscipline where academics parse, critique, and debate the technical details of James's vast corpus of writings. Very little of this literature is accessible to university undergraduates. Moreover, most university psychology instructors (a population whose ranks are increasingly filled by non-PhD adjuncts and part timers) are either only vaguely familiar with or confused about many of James's core concepts such as pragmatism, pluralism, radical empiricism, and his rather peculiar approaches to truth, free will, experience, reality, and religion. Because it is very easy to "get James wrong," most university students end up not getting much of him at all.

This book aims to fill the intellectual gap between the passing paragraph or two dedicated to James in most undergraduate psychology textbooks and the dense academic literature of Jamesian scholars. James never wanted to lend a surname to another ivory tower echo chamber. He was a tireless public lecturer who believed that philosophy should apply to everyday life. If we are to resist the increasing isolation of Jamesian thought to the elite few and bring new generations of curious young minds into the Jamesian conversation, then we need a book that offers students an effective, interesting, and inspiring introduction to William James. This book is intended to do that.

The Book

The book has two goals: (1) to introduce students to the important elements of Jamesian thought and (2) to inspire them to explore that thought further on their own. The book is *not* an analysis or critique of James. However, it does not shy away from highlighting potential weakness or challenges to his thought. By the book's end, students should have a solid grasp of basic Jamesian concepts, including what he meant by radical empiricism, pluralism (or a pluralistic universe), experience (especially the stream of thought), attention, freedom, truth, reality, God, rational belief, moral claims, moral solitude, consciousness, sentiment (how it drives reason), mysticism (or the mystical experience), and pragmatism (or the pragmatic approach). Furthermore, they should understand the interconnections among these concepts and the objections or alternatives to them (for example, monism, determinism, reductionism, idealism, rationalism, etc.).

The book is structured as a dialogue between James and a student. If a teacher is judged by the quality of his students, James is peerless. Socrates had Plato. Plato had Aristotle. Impressive. The list associated with James, however, is nothing short of staggering: George Santayana, Theodore Roosevelt, W. E. B. Du Bois, Gertrude Stein, E. L. Thorndike, Walter Lippman, Morris Cohen, Mary Whiton Calkins, G. Stanley Hall, and more. Men and women who went on to flourishing careers of their own in academics, art, literature, journalism, and politics (Roosevelt not only being president but a Nobel Laureate). How would these students have reacted to James expounding on his ideas of freedom, truth, God, the universe, and the purpose of human existence?

Each chapter envisions James strolling along with one of these famous students discussing a topic. Students are given license to challenge James, disagree, demand examples and clarifications, and generally pose the sort of questions that I hope student readers would have. Given that the context of these conversations is late nineteenth-century Cambridge (Massachusetts), I have striven to balance period rhetoric with the demands of twenty-first-century accessibility. I want to give students some flavor of James's writing, but not at the expense of clarity.

Each chapter follows a similar structure. While walking home, James is confronted by a student with questions or concerns about something James said in lecture. The two decide which road to take (Oxford Street or Divinity Avenue) and the dialogue commences. Each dialogue is preceded by an outline to aid students in following the logical flow as well as a brief biography of the student. Important points in the dialogues are often cued by particular questions, such as "How so . . . ?" "What do you mean by . . . ?" "I'm not sure I follow . . . ?" It is my hope that as they read, students will recognize that a certain question phrasing on the part of the student typically leads to James explaining an important concept.

Occasionally in the dialogues, a rather obvious question arises that James did not specifically address (for example, questions about dualism in chapter 4). On these occasions, I answer as I envision James would have answered holding fast to two guideposts: experience and common sense. My belief is that when in doubt with James, answers grounded in experience and adaptive functioning are most likely to provide credible approximations to what he would have said.

The Man

By 1890, William James had risen to the rank of full professor of philosophy at Harvard University. It was his seventeenth year at the university, and he had only recently moved into a new house, built by his own hand, at 95 Irving Street in Cambridge. Throughout his academic career, James exhibited an exceptional concern for his students—visiting them when they were ill, inviting them to his house for informal get-togethers, and laboring over his lectures to ensure clarity. It wasn't uncommon to see him strolling with students from campus to his home answering questions and elaborating on points of contention. It is in this context that I envision these dialogues. We are the students, walking with James to Irving Street baffled and bemused by the seemingly odd and esoteric positions our mentor has espoused on issues of the human mind, nature of truth, free will, and significance of human existence. We challenge him to make sense of it all. As students of privileged breeding, our sometimes overly bold queries occasionally smack of irreverence, displaying a veneer of knowledge that we parrot more expertly than we understand. James, as always, is generous and patient. He was walking this street when we were but babes and will continue so long after we're gone. It is both a quirk and shame of history that so few were able to share those walks with James and that very likely none of them fully appreciated the gift serendipity bestowed upon them. This book is a feeble attempt to right that wrong. A wider circle should have been granted a step or two with America's most amiable and admirable thinker.

Chapter 1

A Real Fight[1]

Topic: Suicide: Is life worth living?

Student: Theodore Roosevelt

Outline:

Should a rich man commit suicide?
The role of biology in optimistic versus pessimistic personalities
    Natural attentional inclinations
    Consciously directing attention
Review of James's past and struggles with suicide
The origins of suicidal pessimism
    The death of the designer God
    The advantages of a finite God
    Materialistic determinism
Beyond science: taking experience seriously
Choosing freedom
Why life is worth living

Theodore Roosevelt

Theodore Roosevelt was born on October 27, 1858, in New York City. He was a frail child who suffered from asthma. However, as an adult he shared with William James a love of the "strenuous life" of an active outdoorsman (*The Strenuous Life* was also the title of a book he authored in 1901). A year after graduating from Harvard in 1880, Roosevelt was elected to the New York State Assembly. In 1898, Roosevelt served in the Spanish American War as the commander of the "Rough Riders" division and became nationally known as a war hero. He later served as both governor of New York (1899–1900) and president of the United States

---

[1] Taken largely from James's essay "Is life worth living."

(1901–1909). In 1906, he became the first American to win the Nobel Peace Prize for brokering an end to the Russo-Japanese War.

William James sits in a recently emptied lecture hall reviewing some notes. Slowly his attention is drawn to an escalating verbal exchange occurring outside the hall. He tilts his head quizzically trying to decipher the content of the argument from the muffled voices. Then a student enters.

STUDENT: Professor James.

JAMES: Yes.

STUDENT: I think you should come.

JAMES: What's going on?

STUDENT: A bit of a row. Getting somewhat out of hand. Your opinion might help calm things.

JAMES: (gathering his notes) Very well. (Under his breath) Blessed be the peacemakers.

Beneath a cluster of stately arching oak trees, a circle of students is enmeshed in a cacophony of gesticulation and verbal harangue. Among the more agitated combatants is Theodore Roosevelt. A student announces James's arrival on the scene.

STUDENT: Dr. James is here.

Things begin to settle.

JAMES: Gentlemen. Gentlemen!

The group falls into silence.

JAMES: Before this comes to fisticuffs, someone explain to me what the devil's going on?

A bold student steps forward and speaks.

STUDENT: Well . . . a difference of opinion has emerged . . .

JAMES: Clearly . . .

STUDENT: Can we put the issue to you?

JAMES: Of course.

The students exchange nodding glances.

STUDENT: All right. What's your view on this: Does someone of privilege have the right to opt for suicide?

The topic startles James momentarily. He pauses and sighs.

JAMES: Well . . . that's an unexpected question (he begins pacing about, then turns directly at the students). So . . . what we're asking is whether someone blessed with social and economic advantages . . . indeed . . . *despite* these advantages— might he, nonetheless, find himself in such a sad state that he would be justified in tossing all that aside and ending his own life?

ROOSEVELT: (impatient with James's wordiness) Yes. Or put more bluntly, does a rich man have the right to kill himself?

JAMES: (slightly annoyed) Thank you for the clarification, Mr. Roosevelt.

ROOSEVELT: Given his suffering and hopelessness, a poor man might be forgiven for giving up on life . . . but a rich man? No, I see that as a moral weakness.

JAMES: A moral weakness?

SECOND STUDENT: Who are you to pass judgment . . .

THIRD STUDENT: All moral questions involve judgments of one sort or another . . .

Other students jump in, and the argument escalates.

JAMES: Wait. Wait! I think . . . Gentlemen. Gentlemen!

Things slowly settle.

JAMES: I think the heart of the issue isn't so much privilege versus poverty but whether some *right* to suicide can be justified at all. If it can, then it would have to apply uniformly, regardless of one's social status.

The students begin grumbling. Their discontent grows.

JAMES: I propose . . . (raising his voice to quell the rising tide of malcontent) . . . I propose that we more formally take up the issue at my next lecture where we can discuss it in a civilized way. Fair enough?

James scans the group and receives reluctant nods.

JAMES: (with satisfaction) Good. Now, you have other classes and I have a wife and household to return to. So let's all depart in good spirits and meet again tomorrow.

James watches as the students slowly disperse. He commences a leisurely saunter down Divinity Avenue toward his home. Roosevelt watches him depart and then walks briskly to catch up with him.

ROOSEVELT: Professor James.

James stops and turns.

JAMES: Yes. Ahh . . . Mr. Roosevelt.

ROOSEVELT: I wonder if I might have a word with you.

JAMES: Of course. Join me.

They walk on.

JAMES: Am I wrong in presuming that you were at the center of that little ruckus?

ROOSEVELT: I was a bit of an instigator—yes.

JAMES: That role seems to suit you, Mr. Roosevelt.

ROOSEVELT: Instigator?

JAMES: Yes. You seem to relish a good debate.

ROOSEVELT: I suppose that's true.

JAMES: That quality can be a virtue. However, it can be a vice as well if one's goal is to win rather than to learn.

ROOSEVELT: That's a challenge for me.

JAMES: A challenge? What do you mean?

ROOSEVELT: Whatever I do, I tend to do it with vigor. Holding back is not easy for me.

JAMES: In a discussion, Mr. Roosevelt, holding back long enough to understand another's point of view is essential. Otherwise, the discussion is unproductive. It merely becomes a shouting match.

ROOSEVELT: Of course. Sure. But . . .

JAMES: But . . . ?

ROOSEVELT: Well, in this case—given the issue—it seemed to me that passion was warranted.

JAMES: Combatants always believe their passion is warranted, Mr. Roosevelt, though it rarely is.

ROOSEVELT: But Professor James . . . you heard what we were discussing—the value of life itself. If that doesn't fire your blood a bit then I don't know what will.

JAMES: And the fire in your blood told you that life is too valuable to be snuffed out prematurely by one's own hand.

ROOSEVELT: Yes. Yes. Especially if that hand has been blessed with wealth and privilege.

JAMES: I see. But what about personality?

ROOSEVELT: Personality? What do you mean?

JAMES: You're focusing on someone's circumstance—whether they are rich or poor . . . privileged or deprived. But what about someone's internal disposition . . . their personality? Doesn't that also play a role in the value they perceive in living?

ROOSEVELT: Well . . . I suppose . . .

JAMES: (interrupting) Oh, look at that . . .

ROOSEVELT: What?

James points with delight at a squirrel as it races up a sprawling oak tree by the side of the road. To the top it ascends, and then it leaps precariously from one slender waving branch to another.

JAMES: Did you see that?

ROOSEVELT: The squirrel?

JAMES: Yes.

ROOSEVELT: Fun little creatures . . .

JAMES: And quite daring. I'm also convinced that they can be a bit vindictive.

ROOSEVELT: Vindictive? A squirrel?

JAMES: Probably just my imagination . . . but I have two large trees in my front yard and on more than one occasion I've had the distinct impression that the squirrels were casting acorns, quite intentionally, down upon my head, and for what reason I can't say. I've never molested them in any way. Indeed, quite the opposite. I enjoy their company. I fear they don't reciprocate.

ROOSEVELT: (chuckling) Maybe to them you're an intruder.

JAMES: Well . . . we can never be sure how another creature sees the world.

ROOSEVELT: Yes, I recall that from a lecture some weeks ago.

JAMES: Now, getting back to our topic . . .

ROOSEVELT: Yes . . . I believe you accused me of disregarding personality in how one values life.

JAMES: Right . . . often we judge another person on their circumstance. We see someone with wealth and privilege and assume that must bring them happiness . . .

ROOSEVELT: . . . and your point is that one's outlook on life may be more a matter of their internal disposition or personality.

JAMES: Yes. We are often looking externally to understand another person when we should be looking internally.

ROOSEVELT: And personality is more internal than external?

JAMES: Yes. I think one's general outlook on life, be it optimistic or pessimistic, is as much a matter of biology as circumstance.

ROOSEVELT: So we're born to be either jolly or miserable?

JAMES: No, I don't think it's that simple. Do you recall my early lecture on the nature of experience?

ROOSEVELT: Ahh . . . yes, that *stream of thought* that you described.

JAMES: Right.

ROOSEVELT: How does that connect with our biological makeup?

JAMES: That constant stream of sensory inputs always has far more information in it than we can process.

ROOSEVELT: Sure, of course. We can't attend to everything that impinges upon our senses.

JAMES: Right. So we must selectively attend. We focus on *this* rather than *that*. When I noticed the squirrel earlier, I momentarily broke from our conversation. I couldn't do both at once.

ROOSEVELT: And this had something to do with biology?

JAMES: Oh, yes. Our biological makeup exerts a strong influence on our tendency to ignore or attend to various elements in the stream of thought. My natural tendency is to ignore such things as squirrels, birds, trees, and so forth.

ROOSEVELT: Really? But you spotted that squirrel quite readily.

JAMES: Over the years, I have forced myself to pay closer attention to the wonders of nature. It raises my spirits. It's become something of a habit.

ROOSEVELT: You had to force yourself?

JAMES: Yes. When I was younger. I tended to fixate much more on the tragic.

ROOSEVELT: Really. Why so?

JAMES: Good question. Like you, I was born into privileged circumstances. So from your perspective I should have been a happy young man.

ROOSEVELT: And you attribute this to biology . . . to how your biology affected your personality?

JAMES: Oh, yes. I think it played an important role. You see, Mr. Roosevelt, the difference between optimists and pessimists begins with how attention is allocated across that stream of thought. And our biological makeup affects our natural inclination to focus on the hopeful or the glum.

ROOSEVELT: So how do these natural inclinations get written into our biology?

JAMES: Positive experiences give us an excited rush of elevated emotions, so we're naturally attracted to them. At the same time, however, we're also designed to be on guard against mortal threats. Of course, that was much more of an issue in our ancestral past than today. But the tendency remains. Thus, evolution designed our nervous system to be keenly sensitive to both attractive and repulsive signals . . . it's all about survival.

ROOSEVELT: The normally functioning person should be a combination of optimist and pessimist, is that what you're saying?

JAMES: Yes, the potential for either should be there, but being equally balanced is a rarity. All of us tend to lean in one direction or another. In some, it becomes extreme.

ROOSEVELT: For example . . . ?

JAMES: Well . . . take Walt Whitman. His poems sing with such enthusiasm for the glories of nature and life—it's hard to imagine him capable of a solemn mood. Whereas Goethe tells us that in seventy-five years he had but a few weeks free of morbid thoughts. Often whatever initial leaning we have, optimistic or pessimistic, over time it becomes increasingly habitual, and we move evermore to the extreme.

ROOSEVELT: The drift becoming inevitable?

JAMES: Hard to reverse, but not inevitable.

ROOSEVELT: Yes. I agree. It can't be inevitable. I know this for a fact.

JAMES: Oh, how so?

ROOSEVELT: As you said, I was born into great privilege as well . . .

JAMES: You're being modest, Mr. Roosevelt. Your family is one of the wealthiest in the country.

ROOSEVELT: True. But as a child, I was plagued by severe asthma and countless physical ailments. My parents doubted I'd live past four. I had every reason to give up on life.

JAMES: But you didn't.

ROOSEVELT: With my father's encouragement, I found the will to overcome both my physical and spiritual weaknesses.

JAMES: Right. No one's fate is inevitable. Countering our inclinations may be difficult, but not impossible.

ROOSEVELT: And what of yourself . . . if I might inquire? Didn't you earlier concede to a tendency toward pessimism?

JAMES: Indeed.

ROOSEVELT: A tendency that you arrested . . . even reversed?

JAMES: Hmm . . . maybe saying "manage" is the best way to put it.

ROOSEVELT: Then you've been down this road as well.

JAMES: This road . . . ?

ROOSEVELT: Yes. Yes . . . that journey of overcoming one's circumstances . . . overcoming one's self.

JAMES: Ahh . . . yes. I suppose that's true.

ROOSEVELT: May I enquire about that journey? What was the nature of your pessimism and how did you overcome it?

JAMES: Well, explaining that requires delving into the past.

ROOSEVELT: Yes . . . ?

JAMES: But to get there . . . let's start with the present. Who am I to you, right here, right now?

ROOSEVELT: You are Dr. James, professor of philosophy at Harvard University.

JAMES: Would it surprise you to know that I never earned a degree in philosophy . . . or psychology for that matter?

ROOSEVELT: Oh . . . well . . . now that you mention it, I recall hearing that your degree is in medicine.

JAMES: True.

ROOSEVELT: You originally intended to be a doctor?

JAMES: A passing fancy that came and went.

ROOSEVELT: Then why take the degree?

JAMES: I was twenty-seven years old. I was becoming a bit desperate about getting on with my life. My younger brothers were well into their careers—Henry writing for *The Nation* and *Atlantic Monthly*, Wilky and Bob back from the war, working a plantation in Florida—while I seemed to be drifting aimlessly.

ROOSEVELT: I see.

JAMES: So after considerable procrastination, I completed a medical degree even though I had no interest in being a doctor.

ROOSEVELT: What were you interested in?

JAMES: Art.

ROOSEVELT: Art?

JAMES: Yes. As a youngster I wanted to be an artist. Have you ever heard of William Morris Hunt?

ROOSEVELT: Yes . . . the famous painter. You know him?

JAMES: I studied at his studio when I was a teenager.

ROOSEVELT: You must have been talented.

JAMES: I was pretty good. But not good enough.

ROOSEVELT: Well, no one's good enough when they're that young. If you would have stayed with it . . .

JAMES: Staying with it would have meant a conflict . . . with my father.

ROOSEVELT: Oh, he didn't look favorably on an artistic career, I take it.

JAMES: His opposition was . . . indirect. He didn't like the idea, but he didn't want to be domineering. He felt he had too much of that from *his* father. But I knew that he deemed art too . . . sensual. It immersed one too much in the senses . . . the material body. It could stunt one's intellectual and spiritual development, he thought.[1]

ROOSEVELT: Interesting differences between our fathers . . .

JAMES: Oh . . . ?

---

[1] See Feinstein, H. M. (1984). *Becoming William James*. Ithaca, NY: Cornell University Press (pp. 98–99).

ROOSEVELT: My father was very direct and physical . . . but in an encouraging and inspiring way. When I started gasping for air, he would hold me straight up, arms aloft, and command, "Breathe, breathe boy! Breathe in the fresh air. It will strengthen you."

JAMES: Is that right? And it was that encouragement that healed you?

ROOSEVELT: Eventually. When we're young we mostly obey out of respect or fear. Only later do we recognize the love that was there.

JAMES: True. Well . . . whether it was respect or fear . . . or love . . . my father's reservations about art were enough to compel me to abandon it.

ROOSEVELT: I see . . . and is that when you decided on medical school?

JAMES: No. Next, I opted for a career in science. I enrolled at the Lawrence School, here at Harvard.

ROOSEVELT: That pleased your father?

JAMES: For a time . . . until he began thinking that science was too . . . intellectual. It might compromise my spiritual development.

ROOSEVELT: A difficult man to please.

JAMES: Yes, in some ways he could be.

ROOSEVELT: So was it because of your father that you quit science?

JAMES: That was part of it. I also hated chemistry. My family's finances were becoming precarious, and my health turned bad.[2]

ROOSEVELT: Hmm . . .

JAMES: Everything piled on top of me at once . . . or so it seemed.

ROOSEVELT: It was serious.

JAMES: To be frank, at that point in my life I sincerely feared for my sanity.

ROOSEVELT: Really?

JAMES: Attentional focus, Mr. Roosevelt. Combine a natural tendency to fixate on the negative with genuine unpleasant events and one quickly feels overwhelmed and hopeless.

ROOSEVELT: Sounds a bit frightening.

---

[2] Feinstein, p. 155.

JAMES: Yes. So I left. I resigned from the Lawrence School and enrolled in the medical school.

ROOSEVELT: So why didn't you go into practice?

JAMES: I enjoyed learning the physiology . . . and the psychology part—the connection of the mind to the nervous system—all quite fascinating. But dealing with patients. . . . I didn't see myself suited for that. Halfway through my studies I realized I could never be a practicing physician. So there I was again, training for a vocation that I would never fulfill.

ROOSEVELT: But you completed, nonetheless.

JAMES: (chuckling) Not without delays. When it came to delay, I was a master.

ROOSEVELT: What sort of delays?

JAMES: For starters, I accompanied Dr. Agassiz on his expedition to Brazil. We spent a year cataloguing the fauna.

ROOSEVELT: A productive delay at least.

JAMES: To some extent. However, the exoticness of it wore out rather quickly and it ground into excruciation tedium . . . and then I contracted smallpox[3] and went temporarily blind.

ROOSEVELT: Oh my . . .

JAMES: Procrastination sometimes exacts a price. In this case, it was a few weeks in the hospital.

ROOSEVELT: After Brazil, you returned and finished the degree?

JAMES: Oh . . . no, no. My bad health and depressed mental state required convalescing—or so I convinced my father. I next went off to Europe . . . Germany mostly . . . some recovery, some study.

ROOSEVELT: Is that when you learned to speak German?

JAMES: No, no. I learned German . . . and French in my childhood. I schooled in Europe when I was a boy. France . . . Germany . . . England . . . the whole family spent time in Europe, my father thought *cosmopolitanism* was essential to a proper upbringing.

ROOSEVELT: I see. So you recovered in Germany after returning from Brazil and then back to Cambridge finally to finish the degree.

JAMES: Yes . . . finally. To complete the unwanted degree.

---

[3] Technically varioloid, a milder form of the disease; see Feinstein, p. 174.

ROOSEVELT: But didn't the degree lead to teaching here at Harvard?

JAMES: Not directly. I was once again hit with that sense of being overwhelmed. So I drifted . . . again.

ROOSEVELT: I see. What sort of drifting?

JAMES: I read a lot, avoided all vocational commitments . . . and (he pauses and scans the skies) sunk deeper and deeper into a sense of uselessness.

ROOSEVELT: Uselessness? With all the experience and knowledge you had acquired? How could that be useless?

JAMES: Experience . . . ? Knowledge . . . ? Of what value are they if you have no inkling how to apply them?

ROOSEVELT: I see.

JAMES: Is life really worth living? I wondered. Have *you* ever pondered that question?

ROOSEVELT: No. Not in any serious way.

JAMES: Why do you think people opt against suicide?

ROOSEVELT: Well . . . I guess I'm more of an optimist by disposition. Good will follow bad eventually if one persists.

JAMES: Yes. Faith in the future can provide one with strength. And of course, there's the religious injunction: Thou shalt not kill. I imagine that dissuades more than a few from seriously considering suicide.

ROOSEVELT: Yes, I agree. It seems to me that the fear of dying along with the hope of a better future are compelling reasons to not give up. Honestly, I struggle to understand why anyone would want to die.

JAMES: So even if one fell abruptly from the merriment of privilege to the misery of poverty, you'd encourage him to be brave and push on.

ROOSEVELT: Most likely.

JAMES: But don't you agree that if that encouragement is to be convincing, there must be more to it than just "thou shalt not kill"?

ROOSEVELT: We should provide all possible reasons we can muster.

JAMES: And our reasons are most effective if they directly target the cause of the despondency, don't you think?

ROOSEVELT: It would seem so.

JAMES: So first we must understand the pessimism. What are its origins? What does the pessimist focus on in his experience that produces the dark sickness in his soul?

ROOSEVELT: Yes.

JAMES: Here's what I think, Mr. Roosevelt. I think that suicidal pessimism arises from the glaring contrast between the world as we once understood it and the world as we know it now.

ROOSEVELT: I'm not sure I follow.

JAMES: The modern scientific view of the world breeds hopelessness in a way unknown to past generations.

ROOSEVELT: How so?

JAMES: Life is and always has been a duality.

ROOSEVELT: Duality? What do you mean?

JAMES: Joy and sorrow linked together. Nature is indescribably beautiful and immeasurably cruel at the same time. Compassion and brutality, love and hate, hope and despair—life is constantly presenting both to us. Our ancestors knew this just as we know it today.

ROOSEVELT: True enough.

JAMES: But past generations could reconcile the darker side of life as being the result of man's sinful nature. A loving God did not intend for there to be such evil. Eden was our destiny until we ruined it by disobedience. There was perfection in God's original design of nature, only later spoiled by man's ambition.

ROOSEVELT: That's how past generations explained pain and suffering—is that what you're saying?

JAMES: Yes.

ROOSEVELT: And that logic no longer holds?

JAMES: An evolutionary understanding of the world reveals a fatal flaw in that myth. There was never any perfection in nature's original design. It always has been an ugly struggle for existence. The beauty we detect in nature is purely functional. A flower or song attracts so that seeds might be spread or prey devoured. The suffering and predation we witness long predates humanity. It was written into nature from the start.

ROOSEVELT: So evolution disproves the existence of a loving God.

JAMES: Hmm . . . some have drawn that conclusion. I'm not convinced of that. But I *am* convinced that it disproves the simplistic notion of a designer God—a God who intentionally designed a perfect world only to have it corrupted by man.

ROOSEVELT: So how does the death of the designer God contribute to suicidal pessimism?

JAMES: In a world designed by God, one can always find consolation in the thought that present evils will ultimately be overcome by God's justice. Injustice and suffering are man's creations. But in the end, God will set it right.

ROOSEVELT: That's the hope of many religious believers.

JAMES: But that hope is dashed.

ROOSEVELT: It is?

JAMES: If the universe was flawed from the start, then there's no original state of perfection to which it can be set aright. Injustice and suffering were not introduced into the world by man, they were there from the beginning.

ROOSEVELT: I see.

JAMES: But it goes even deeper than just this.

ROOSEVELT: Even deeper? What do you mean?

JAMES: It seems to me that if evil was part of creation from the very start, then that not only disproves the presence of a designer God but also calls into question an infinitely powerful one.

ROOSEVELT: You think God cannot be all powerful if evil has always been present?

JAMES: If he were, why did he not banish evil from the start rather than letting it take root and grow?

ROOSEVELT: I think that's an issue that theologians have been wrestling with for centuries.

JAMES: Yes, indeed. It was one that my father wrestled with as well, for years. He was a theologian . . . of a rather unorthodox sort.

ROOSEVELT: Did he arrive at any conclusions?

JAMES: In the end, he was drawn to the idea of a finite God—an idea to which I'm sympathetic.

ROOSEVELT: A finite God?

JAMES: Yes. A God whose goodness and power are great—far greater than ours, but not infinite.

ROOSEVELT: That's not the typical Christian view of God.

JAMES: No. Not at all. But I think there's a great advantage to this notion. It offers an appealing emancipation.

ROOSEVELT: Emancipation?

JAMES: There was a stifling Calvinist strain of thinking passed along in my family—starting with my grandfather.

ROOSEVELT: Calvinism?

JAMES: Yes, that old Protestant idea of predestination—that God has strictly arranged everything as it was meant to be, leaving no room for any deviation from that original divine plan.

ROOSEVELT: Why is a divine plan stifling?

JAMES: Because it left us no room for freedom. All that *is*, *was*, and ever *will be* was determined from the dawn of time by an infinite, all powerful God. If you suffer misfortune—then it was meant to be. All your triumphs and tragedies are exactly what God intended for you since long before you were born and nothing you do can alter that.

ROOSEVELT: Which fits with the Calvinist idea of predestination—some have been chosen by God for salvation and others have not.

JAMES: Yes. But if God is finite, predestination is replaced by uncertainty. Even God doesn't know exactly where the universe is heading, and this fits with what we know of evolution.

ROOSEVELT: So rather than a predestined universe we live in an evolving universe.

JAMES: Precisely . . . and what do we know of evolution?

ROOSEVELT: It's not entirely predictable.

JAMES: Right. An evolving universe is potentially open to novelty. It may take unexpected paths. If this is so; if the universe is truly free, then one's choices really *do* have meaning. Your actions have consequences not only for your own salvation but also for that of the universe.

ROOSEVELT: For the universe? What do you mean?

JAMES: If God is finite . . . if he is powerful, but not all powerful . . . then maybe part of our destiny as humans is to help God bring about the world's redemption.

Maybe God needs us as much as we need him. Our actions are important because we must work with God to save the world. God can't do it alone.

ROOSEVELT: So you're saying that our lives have purpose because we are meant to help God save the world?

JAMES: Yes. This is another reason why I've grown to prefer the idea of a finite God over an infinite one.

ROOSEVELT: All right, so we banish the all-powerful universe-designing Calvinist God of predestination, and in doing so we gain freedom and with this freedom our choices, actions, our very lives obtain a meaning they didn't have before.

JAMES: Yes, I think an evolutionary understanding of the world leads us to this conclusion.

ROOSEVELT: I'm sure that my atheist friends would demand more than just banishing the Calvinist God. Evolution doesn't just show us that God is finite. It shows us that God is dead. Why not get rid of God entirely and instead say our lives have meaning because we must use science to save the world?

JAMES: No. Taking that path will never work. If we go strictly with science; if we let *it* be our God, then we fall into a view of life no less miserable than Calvinism.

ROOSEVELT: Truly? How so? Wasn't it evolution that opened our eyes to a universe free of predestination?

JAMES: Yes. Free of predestination. But science trades predestination for even more intolerable prison.

ROOSEVELT: What's that?

JAMES: Materialistic determinism.

ROOSEVELT: Materialistic determinism?

James Yes.

ROOSEVELT: What is that?

JAMES: From a strictly scientific perspective, the freedom we see in the evolutionary process is an illusion. Look for a moment at the tree leaves fluttering in the wind. Would you say that in the next moment you could predict with certainty how the leaves' fluttering will change?

ROOSEVELT: Well . . . in a roundabout way . . . but with certainty? No.

JAMES: Of course not. The breeze could shift, a bird might suddenly perch upon the branch, a raindrop might weigh one or two of them down in a way you could not have known a moment prior.

ROOSEVELT: And thus, the course of leaf fluttering is not entirely predictable.

JAMES: Correct. And that unpredictability could easily be mistaken for freedom. However, it is not.

ROOSEVELT: How so?

JAMES: The unpredictable patterns of flutter are still entirely determined by the laws of physics. The leaf changed its movement from one moment to the next, not because it was free to do as it willed but because when the breeze changed, or the bird perched, or the raindrop landed, the variables affecting the applicable laws changed . . . but the laws still applied, and the leaf followed.

ROOSEVELT: So if we could somehow have understood how the laws of motion were affected by those changes, we could have predicted the leaf's next move. What on the surface seems unpredictable is really a matter of our ignorance, not of a true *inability to predict*.

JAMES: Exactly. This is what science tells us. When we look at the evolutionary process, we see something complex beyond imagination, like watching a billion leaves on a million trees with winds swirling about, birds and downpours coming and going, leaving no possibility of predictive certainty.

ROOSEVELT: Yet all of it just as subject to the laws of physics as a billiard game at the local pub.

JAMES: Correct.

ROOSEVELT: So we replace the Calvinist God with the God of Science and what are we left with?

JAMES: Materialistic Determinism. Dumb matter blindly following the laws of physics.

ROOSEVELT: I see. And this includes us, as well?

JAMES: Yes. We're composed of matter, after all. The brain is a material organ . . . cells and chemicals.

ROOSEVELT: Right.

JAMES: Remember earlier I told you of my drifting years after I received my MD but failed to go into practice?

ROOSEVELT: Yes. You said it was then that you seriously question the value of existence.

JAMES: Right. It was a time when I came closest to suicide.

ROOSEVELT: And . . . materialistic determinism played some role in this?

JAMES: My reading of science provided no way out from the disheartening reality that our choices aren't real, and our actions are inconsequential. Science had given us a god more diabolical and tyrannical then the Calvinists could ever have imagined.

ROOSEVELT: Really? How so?

JAMES: Tyrannical—because as with the Calvinistic God, all that presently is, was determined by past circumstance. The universe unfolds according to the dictates of nature's laws. Not predictable from a human standpoint, but just as utterly determined as the predestined universe of the Designer God.

ROOSEVELT: And diabolical?

JAMES: Because along with this undeniable determinism is an overwhelming sense of freedom. The leaves look free! My choices seem free! Yet nothing in science can support such a belief. The brain is a material substance, subject to the laws of nature just as surely as the breeze and leaves. Every thought and action of mine have been in nature's cards from the very first hand.

ROOSEVELT: You mentioned earlier that today we have reasons for despair unknown to past generations . . .

JAMES: Right! And materialistic determinism is chief among them. Science has provided us with comforts and inventions that have made the life of the body more secure and pleasurable than in any previous age. But the life of the soul has been emptied to a wasteland . . . and anyone brave enough to face honestly this wasteland can hardly be blamed for questioning the point of it all. That's certainly what I did.

ROOSEVELT: What pulled you back from the abyss?

JAMES: Hmmm . . . that is curious question. How shall I explain . . . .?

James looks skyward momentarily lost in thought. The answer is fraught with a lifetime of complication. How to simplify? He wonders.

JAMES: Are you familiar with the line: "I am one who has loved not wisely, but too well."

ROOSEVELT: (pauses, thinking) Othello—isn't it?

JAMES: Yes. A fateful choice he made: to take the life, not of himself, but of his loving and chaste wife, Desdemona.

ROOSEVELT: There's no tragedy like a Shakespearean tragedy.

JAMES: And . . . you would agree, would you not, that the taking of a life is a momentous choice. Not to be done in haste.

ROOSEVELT: Most certainly.

JAMES: Wasn't that Othello's great error? Believing his knowledge of Desdemona was complete, when in fact, his ignorance was far wider.

ROOSEVELT: Are you saying that you began to fear that by taking your own life, you might be making Othello's error?

JAMES: Yes. I began to wonder if the profound, undisputable experience we have of free will might not be telling us that our understanding of the universe is still badly incomplete. Maybe we need more than just science to understand the world.

ROOSEVELT: So what source of knowledge do you call upon if you want to go beyond science—philosophy . . . religion?

JAMES: Well . . . yes, but I think all the academic labels we use merely describe different forms of experience. We have scientific experiences, religious experiences, intellectual experiences, social . . . literary experiences. We need to take all of them seriously.

ROOSEVELT: And if we take them seriously, what are they telling us?

JAMES: In none of them, not even our scientific experiences, do we feel as if we are reading off some prefabricated script, our roles and destinies cosmically ordained by God or physics. (shaking his fist) Instead, doesn't life feel much more like a fight—a *real* fight where something eternal is in the balance? [4]

ROOSEVELT: (excitedly) Yes! Precisely. That is how I always felt.

JAMES: And isn't it also in the midst of a fight . . . a struggle . . . that we are often at our best.

ROOSEVELT: Yes!

JAMES: Boethius wrote his most triumphant philosophy while in prison. The pinnacle of Hebrew scripture was achieved in exile, not during the glories of Solomon.

ROOSEVELT: So you're convinced that our experience of freedom is not an illusion.

JAMES: Yes. That pervasive sense of freedom that we experience; it is so deeply a part of us . . . so definitively human, that it compels us to . . . at the very least, *hypothesize* that our science is incomplete. It may be that conscious awareness places limits on determinism.

ROOSEVELT: How so?

---

[4] James's actual quote is too good not to cite: "If this life be not a real fight in which something is eternally gained for the universe by success, it is no better than a game of private theatricals from which we may withdraw at will. It feels like a fight."

JAMES: Think of what I can do with my mind—the odd ability I have to deliberately hold one idea in my awareness when I could hold a different . . . completely opposite idea. Even while knowing all the scientific evidence for determinism, I can still choose to think that freedom is real. I can't convince myself that that choice is insignificant.

ROOSEVELT: So believing in free will makes it a reality?

JAMES: Yes. And my first act of freedom was to choose to believe that it existed and live accordingly. In my darkest hour, it was this realization that saved me.

ROOSEVELT: But is it true? Could you not be accused of just wishful thinking?

JAMES: Wishful . . . ? Maybe? But it is not *unreasonable* thinking. The opposite conclusion relies no less on unproven hypotheses, for it requires that we deny our most basic experience of life—that our choices matter.

ROOSEVELT: So if you were to counsel someone, rich man or poor man, who was on the precipice of suicide, what advice would you give? How can you convince someone that life is worth living?

JAMES: Hmm . . . a difficult challenge. What would I say . . . ? (James ponders for moment) I'd start by trying to convince him that he does not have to be controlled by his pessimistic inclinations. We are free to choose the way we see our circumstance. We can train ourselves to focus more on our blessings than on our woes.

ROOSEVELT: In the way that you trained yourself to focus on the beauty of nature.

JAMES: Yes. Exactly. If novelty is real and determinism is the illusion, then we can shape novel, different . . . *better* forms of ourselves.

ROOSEVELT: And then there is the importance of each human life . . .

JAMES: Yes. Yes. How we each have a role to play in saving the world . . . making it a better place. Nothing is preordained. The present moment's gloom does not necessarily mean the future will be the same.

ROOSEVELT: And our actions make a difference in how the future plays out.

JAMES: Yes. God needs our help, but others—friends, family, one's country and community—they need our help as well. Life *is* worth living. And from that belief, the reality will take root.

Chapter 2

What Is Real?[1]

Topic: The nature of experience and the construction of reality

Student: Walter Lippmann

Outline:

Lippmann challenges James's idea that "experience is reality"
    The meaning of "real"
    The difference between reality and accuracy
    The inconsequential nature of unexperienced causes
    Is an unconscious universe real?

Understanding the science of experience
    The failure of reductionism
    The five features of experience
    The 'I' of experience
    The conceptual limiting of experience
Pure experience

Walter Lippmann

Walter Lippmann was born on September 23, 1889, in New York City. He earned his BA from Harvard in 1909, where he was heavily influenced by both William James and George Santayana. He went on to have an over sixty-year career as a journalist, commentator, and author. In 1914, he helped found the *New Republic* magazine, which continues to be an important influence in society and politics. He also wrote for the *World*, the *Washington Post*, and the *New York Herald*,

---

[1] Largely taken from James, W. (1905). The thing and its relations. *Journal of Philosophy, 2*(2); Myers, G. E. (1986). *William James: His life and thought.* New Haven, CT: Yale University Press (chapters 2 and 11); James, W. (1890). *The principles of psychology.* New York: Henry Holt (chapters 9–12, 21); Krueger, J. W. (2006). The varieties of pure experience: William James and Kitaro Nishida on consciousness and embodiment. *William James Studies, 1.* http://www.jstor.org/stable/26203679.

earning two Pulitzer Prizes in 1958 and 1962. Lippmann's writings were highly regarded by President Woodrow Wilson, who used them as a framework for his fourteen-point resettlement plan after World War I and for the establishment of the League of Nations. Lippmann briefly served as assistant secretary of war in the Wilson administration, where he took part in the negotiations leading to the Treaty of Versailles. In his most influential book, *Public Opinion* (1922), he warned against the inability of the average citizen to reasonably judge issues when mass media coverage reduced them to mere slogans.

LIPPMANN: Professor James . . . Professor James!

James pauses and turns to see a student, Walter Lippmann, hastily approaching. With furrowed brow, James jabs a figure at the student.

JAMES: Walter . . . right?

LIPPMANN: Oh . . . right. I'm Walter. Walter Lippmann.

JAMES: Yes . . . I thought so.

LIPPMANN: I wonder if I could have a word with you. Umm . . . something you said earlier in lecture . . . it left me confused.

JAMES: Confusion can be the first step to enlightenment.

LIPPMANN: Right . . . sure. Well, you see . . .

JAMES: (scanning off into the distance) Oxford or Divinity?

LIPPMANN: Ahh . . . what? I'm not sure . . .

JAMES: (turning his attention back to Lippmann) I'm on my way home. I presume you're walking with me. Should we take Oxford Street or Divinity Avenue? Either works for me, but I thought you might have a preference.

LIPPMANN: Oh . . . well, no, not really, no preference. Actually . . . Oxford is more picturesque.

JAMES: Oxford . . .

LIPPMANN: Ahh . . . but, well, Divinity puts me closer to my flat.

JAMES: Divinity, then.

LIPPMANN: But . . . well, no . . . if you prefer Oxford, then don't let me . . .

JAMES: I prefer getting home before dark.

LIPPMANN: Oh . . . right . . .

JAMES: Divinity.

LIPPMANN: That's fine. Thank you.

They begin a casual saunter down Divinity Avenue.

JAMES: Now . . . you were confused about something?

LIPPMANN: Well . . . just before the lecture ended, you said something about . . . something to the effect that . . . well, if I heard you correctly . . . ahh . . . *experience is reality*. Is that right?

JAMES: Yes. Exactly.

LIPPMANN: I'm not entirely sure how to understand that.

JAMES: Hmmm. Well, I'm not entirely sure how to state it more clearly. Experience is reality. If you experience it, it's real. If you don't, it isn't.

LIPPMANN: It's just . . . that seems a bit . . . too simplistic.

JAMES: (pointing at a tree) See that tree over there.

LIPPMANN: Yes.

JAMES: Walk through it.

LIPPMANN: (embarrassed chuckling) Well . . . of course, that's impossible.

JAMES: Right. Because it's real. You see it. You experience it. It's a real tree. If you try to walk through it, you'll just get a ripe bruise on your head. Now see that tree over there? (James points down the open road)

LIPPMANN: (a bit confused) Well . . . no . . . that's just the road.

JAMES: Right . . . you don't experience a tree over that way. It's just imaginary. It's not real. Experience is reality. Make sense now?

LIPPMANN: But aren't there many things we experience that aren't real?

JAMES: Such as . . . ?

LIPPMANN: Well . . . how about a mirage? Suppose I'm wandering through the desert, delirious from heat and thirst, and I mistakenly see a waterhole off in the distance. I race toward the hole, thinking I have found my salvation, only to find nothing, just more sand and scorched earth. That seems to be an obvious case where my experience wasn't real.

JAMES: No, I'd say your experience corresponded exactly to your reality.

LIPPMANN: How is that possible when my experience told me there was a waterhole and, in fact, there wasn't?

JAMES: I said that experience was reality. I didn't say that experience was always *accurate*.

LIPPMANN: I suppose that is the crux of my confusion. Doesn't experience have to be accurate to be real?

JAMES: What do you mean by real?

LIPPMANN: Well . . . I guess real means . . . something that objectively exists . . . out there . . . in the world.

JAMES: Okay. So *real* is the same as *objectively existing*—correct?

LIPPMANN: Yes. That sounds right.

JAMES: Hmm . . . Walter . . . ?

LIPPMANN: Yes . . . ?

JAMES: Reach into your pocket. I presume you have a bill or two of currency.

LIPPMANN: You're in need of a loan?

JAMES: No. I'm in need of an *objectively existing* thing that isn't *real*.

LIPPMANN: Okay . . . (he reaches into his pocket and produces a one dollar note) Are you going to tell me my dollar isn't real?

James reaches into the breast pocket of his suit coat and produces some lecture notes.

JAMES: No, no. It's real enough. So are my lecture notes. But you would agree that they *really* aren't the same—right?

LIPPMANN: Of course.

JAMES: If toss my notes into the street, it's unlikely anyone would give them a glance.

LIPPMANN: Hmm . . . maybe a student worried about his grade, but I take your point. To most, they're nothing more than just scribblings on paper.

JAMES: Of no appreciable value . . .

LIPPMANN: Agreed.

JAMES: But throw your dollar in the street and a fight could ensue.

LIPPMANN: Sure, men will fight over what they believe is valuable.

JAMES: Indeed. In fact, I would contend that more blood has been spilled in the history of mankind over that note you're carrying than just about anything else we've conjured up.

LIPPMANN: Likely true.

JAMES: But why? Look at them. (James grabs the dollar from Lippmann's hand and shakes it along with the lecture notes) They are both just scribblings on paper . . . objectively there's no difference between them. Yet we kill for one and regard the other as litter in the street.

LIPPMANN: But the difference is obvious. One has a value that the other doesn't. I can buy food or lodging with my dollar. You can do none of those with your notes.

JAMES: Right. One *really* has value and the other doesn't. But why? Is there something about the paper or scribblings on your note that necessarily make it valuable, while mine is worthless?

LIPPMANN: Well . . . it's a social agreement . . .

JAMES: Imagine tomorrow the government announced, "toss out those dollar bills you've been carrying, Harvard lecture notes have become the official currency of the nation."

LIPPMANN: Well . . . I suppose that . . . suddenly you've become a rich man.

JAMES: Indeed. Lucky me. Reality has changed to my advantage.

LIPPMANN: I think I'm grasping your point. You're saying that the *reality* of something doesn't necessarily correspond to its objective existence. Is that right?

JAMES: Spot on, Walter. Objectively, there's no reason why your paper is more valuable than mine. But we *experience* yours as valuable and mine as not.

LIPPMANN: So if real doesn't mean . . . existing objectively, what does it mean?

JAMES: Good question. Let's revisit your mirage.

LIPPMANN: Yes. I recall you claimed that my experience corresponded exactly with my reality, even though my experience turned out to be inaccurate.

JAMES: Right. I made that claim because you told me that when you saw the waterhole off in the distance, you regarded it as your salvation and, if I may add a touch of drama, you then *clawed* your way desperately to it expecting to find relief from your blinding thirst.

LIPPMANN: Right . . . only to find it was nothing but a sun-induced illusion.

JAMES: I maintain that at the moment you first experienced the waterhole, it was real . . . very real.

LIPPMANN: But it wasn't there.

JAMES: A fact you uncovered later. But let's stick with the moment of the encounter. Your experience of the waterhole was real because it produced very *real* effects.

LIPPMANN: Effects?

JAMES: Yes. Your mental attitude changed. Prior to the encounter, you thought yourself doomed. After it, you thought you were saved.

LIPPMANN: I see . . .

JAMES: Your motor actions also changed—from aimless wandering to a goal-directed trajectory. You made deliberate haste to the waterhole.

LIPPMANN: So you're saying that my experience of the waterhole was real because it affected me. It changed my thoughts and actions.

JAMES: That's it. Reality means effectiveness. Something is real if it has the power to cause. The waterhole was real because it caused changes in you. Money . . . *value* . . . are real because they affect how people think and behave.

LIPPMANN: But the waterhole turned out to be a mirage . . .

JAMES: Right, and that was revealed to you because of—experience. As you drew closer to the spot where the hole was supposed to be and no water was found, you realized that your earlier experience was in error. Your reality changed. The water-hole no longer had any power to affect you.

LIPPMANN: So your definition of *real* is anything that has the power to cause.

JAMES: Correct.

LIPPMANN: But can't there be causes that completely escape our experience?

JAMES: Sure.

LIPPMANN: Well . . . if there are causes that escape our experience and by defini-tion those causes are real, then how can reality be limited to our experience?

JAMES: You're an excellent student, Walter. I predict you'll go far in life. Yes, tech-nically speaking reality is more than just our experience. But that is an observation that is of no consequence. For all practical purposes . . . for all matters that make a difference in life . . . it might as well be the case that *experience is reality.*

LIPPMANN: Well . . . forgive me, Professor James . . . and with all due respect . . . but . . . isn't that a bit glib. You admit you're wrong—that reality is *more* than just our experience, but you claim it doesn't matter.

JAMES: That's right.

James smiles and begins whistling a jaunty little tune. Lippmann is crestfallen as his admiration for James sinks into bitter disappointment. James senses this.

JAMES: Look . . . let's plumb the matter more deeply. Give me an example of an unexperienced cause, and let's see where it goes.

LIPPMANN: Alright . . . (Lippmann sighs, thinking) . . . Let's suppose . . . okay . . . okay. . . . . . Let's suppose I'm on safari in the jungles of Africa.

JAMES: Interesting . . .

LIPPMANN: . . . And I unknowingly ingest a dangerous parasite.

JAMES: Hmm . . .

LIPPMANN: The parasite acts slowly, so it's not until days later that I come down with symptoms—fever, intestinal cramps . . . diarrhea . . .

JAMES: (interrupting) Spare me the ugly details, I get the idea.

LIPPMANN: Something very real has affected me. But nothing in my experience can identify it. So there's a reality out there, an unknown parasite, that transcends my experience. Therefore, reality is not *just* experience.

JAMES: Sounds good. Aristotle would be proud. But let's think a moment. When you came down with the rather unpleasant symptoms, what did you do?

LIPPMANN: I imagine that I . . . confined myself to bed . . . maybe sought out a physician . . .

JAMES: Good. Good. And when you sought out that physician, he likely inquired about your past behavior—no?

LIPPMANN: What do you mean?

JAMES: He asked you such things as, "Where have you been?" "What have you eaten?" "Did you perchance fill your canteen with river water?" Inquiries such as these.

LIPPMANN: I imagine so. He would want to identify the cause of my illness.

JAMES: In other words, a good doctor would ask you to reflect on your experience in order to better isolate the reason . . . the cause . . . *the reality* behind your sickness.

LIPPMANN: Yes . . . ?

JAMES: Your experience would reveal *reality* to him . . . and to you. That reality being the likely cause of what made you ill.

LIPPMANN: Okay . . . ?

JAMES: Let's suppose that you reveal to him that you did, in fact, fill your canteen with river water and drink it.

LIPPMANN: Well . . . fine but I still could not reveal the actual cause of my illness. I had the experience of drinking water, not of ingesting a parasite.

JAMES: Yes. True. However, upon hearing that you drank the water he might announce, "Ahh . . . yes. We've had several reports of that recently. People drinking from the river and then becoming ill, just like you."

LIPPMANN: So we—the doctor and I—are likely to attribute the cause to contaminated water, not a parasite of which neither of us is yet familiar.

JAMES: The reality that you and the doctor agree upon is that which you experienced. That being one where contaminated water caused intestinal distress.

LIPPMANN: But that leaves it rather vague, doesn't it?

JAMES: Sometimes reality is vague. But I take your point. Our good doctor may be quite dissatisfied with stopping the inquiry there. He may want to know the precise nature of the contamination.

LIPPMANN: Yes. So he takes water samples.

JAMES: We can imagine him burning the midnight oil in some primitive colonial laboratory examining water samples under a microscope, eventually finding our tiny wiggling culprit. Six months hence from your brush with death, he may write you of the great discovery, saying, "Now we know the deeper reality of the situation. It was this wiggly-squiggly thing living in the river."

LIPPMANN: A great medical advance.

JAMES: But how did this advance occur? Did it not require an *experience*?!

LIPPMANN: Well, yes . . . I guess so. Using his microscope, he experienced the parasite in a way that was impossible before.

JAMES: And with that new experience, a new reality dawned. And with it our way of thinking and behaving regarding intestinal distress while on safari changed. No more cold compresses and bed rest. Instead we have this foul-tasing substance, quinine, you can take to rid yourself of the parasite.

LIPPMANN: Makes sense, I guess.

JAMES: But you can't have the new reality and the new effect until you have the experience. If our good doctor had never experienced the parasite, then we continue to exist in a reality where contaminated water is the cause of intestinal distress, and we continue treating it with bed rest and cold compresses.

LIPPMANN: So one could say that the *real* cause of intestinal distress is parasitic infection. But until we experience that cause, *our reality*, the reality that dictates our behavior, is one where contaminated water is the cause.

JAMES: Right. And until we discover . . . or experience parasites, the "contaminated water" reality is the only one that matters.

LIPPMANN: I see . . .

JAMES: In fact, I'll go even further along these lines. Let's imagine an entire universe where experience is lacking.

LIPMANN: Where experience is lacking?

JAMES: Yes. Where no beings exist capable of having conscious experiences such as ours.

LIPPMANN: You're speaking of a universe of nothing but dead matter.

JAMES: Yes. A vast, swirling mass of planets, stars, and galaxies, all afire with the push and pull of physical forces clumping and dispersing matter about over inexhaustible eons of time.

LIPPMANN: Such as our universe was before any life emerged.

JAMES: Yes. Exactly. Now . . . does that universe exist?

LIPPMANN: Of course it does. Our universe existed long before humans ever arrived on the scene.

JAMES: And so you'd say that that universe was real. Correct?

LIPPMANN: Well . . . of course it's real. It has causal power. It ultimately had the power to cause us!

JAMES: But what if it never did?

LIPPMAN: What if it never caused us or any other living conscious being?

JAMES: Yes.

LIPPMANN: Would it be *real* in that case?

JAMES: Yes. That's what I'm asking.

LIPPMANN: Yes . . . no . . . I'm not sure.

JAMES: It's a dilemma. But it's a dilemma that doesn't matter. Think about it. It's a universe that *no one . . . nothing* has ever experienced. No one . . . nothing ever knew it existed. So who cares whether it's real or not. Its existence or not . . . it's reality or not, is of no consequence. It might as well not be real. It might as well never have existed.

LIPPMANN: For matter to *matter*, it must be experienced.

JAMES: (nodding) That's the nub of it.

Lippmann falls momentarily silent, taking it all in.

LIPPMANN: I supposed then . . . ?

JAMES: . . . Yes . . . ?

LIPPMANN: The great significance you place on experience . . . ?

JAMES: Yes . . . ?

LIPPMANN: I suppose that is why you and others have defined psychology as the scientific study of experience.

JAMES: Yes. I think so. (he turns on Lippmann with a bit of scowl) It's just a pity that most of the others have become so fixated on the *science* part that they've badly botched the *experience* part.

LIPPMANN: Oh . . . ? What do you mean?

JAMES: The *science* of experience. Impressive sounding, isn't it?

LIPPMANN: I suppose so.

JAMES: Coined by impressive, austere-looking men eager for psychologists to gain the same prestige afforded to physicists and chemists.

LIPPMANN: Well . . . I think they want to be seen as scientists in equal regard as those others.

JAMES: Right . . . so in seeking this regard the emphasis of our discipline must be on the science . . . the methodology with which we attack our subject.

LIPPMANN: Of course. If we are to have a science of experience, then we must apply rigorous scientific methods to the topic.

JAMES: And what is the key element of rigorous scientific methods?

LIPPMANN: Key element . . . ? Well, I suppose the control of variables so that proper cause and effect relationships can be uncovered.

JAMES: Right . . . good. So to control these variables, we must identify them, isolate one from another, and test each one's effect separately . . . and so forth.

LIPPMANN: Right.

JAMES: Notice the reductionistic thinking necessary to apply this approach. What you intend to study must be broken down into its fundamental components so that those components can be isolated, manipulated, and analyzed.

LIPPMANN: Sure . . . that's how good science works.

JAMES: Fine . . . if you're dealing with chemistry or physics. But reductionism fails when applied to experience.

LIPPMANN: Why so? Doesn't experience ultimately reduce to matter and physical forces, just like anything else in the universe?

JAMES: Well . . . that was the assumption that held sway in the earliest schools of psychology. But it's badly mistaken. Experience is irreducible. Breaking it down into constituent parts destroys the very thing you're trying to study—experience.

LIPPMANN: Destroys it?

JAMES: Yes. It turns it into something that is *not* experience.

LIPPMANN: Into what?

JAMES: An objective description of matter and physical forces. But that is not what we experience.

James can see that Lippmann isn't grasping what he's trying to convey.

JAMES: (pointing to treetop) See that beautiful red bird in the tree over there.

LIPPMANN: Oh, yes. Very pretty.

JAMES: It is pretty. Raises your spirits just to see it. It also makes me curious . . . too small to be a cardinal, I think. Seems too early in the year to be seeing such birds.

LIPPMANN: And so . . . what does the bird have to do with the notion that reductionism destroys experience?

JAMES: I'll show you. Let's be good scientists and reduce our experience of the red bird in the tree to its fundamental components.

LIPPMANN: Okay . . . ?

JAMES: What I'm really seeing . . . according to reductionism . . . is longer wavelength light energy reflecting off an oblong surface positioned at a certain angular vector relative to my head, set against a broader context of various short, midrange, and otherwise variable wavelengths.

LIPPMANN: I suppose . . . I'm not entirely sure . . .

JAMES: What I've given you is a rough physical description of the light energy striking the retinal surface of my eye. That's what the bird experience *really is*, if I reduce it to its fundamental properties.

LIPPMANN: I don't think the early schools of psychology—Wundt's Voluntarism or Titchener's Structuralism—were quite going to that level of reduction.

JAMES: True enough . . . they were more content with intensities, input modalities, angles, and so forth. But the approach is the same and the folly just as ruinous.

LIPPMANN: How so?

JAMES: Because none of that captures my experience of seeing the bird—how it feels *to me* to be in its presence or hear its song . . . what memories it evokes or future hopes it stirs. I could give you a complete chemical description of lemon juice and tell you that's what your mouth *actually encounters* when you bite into a lemon, and that wouldn't give you the first clue as what biting into a lemon feels like.

LIPPMANN: I see. So experience must be taken as a whole . . .

JAMES: Holistically and subjectively. Objective, reductionistic methods are useless when applied to a holistic, subjective phenomenon.

LIPPMANN: So if objective, reductionistic methods fail to capture experience, how then can it be studied?

JAMES: I don't think we have an adequate answer to that question yet. New methods need to be developed. The best I can propose at this point is some form of holistic introspection, where we reflect upon the content of our experience while preserving that content's integrity. Whatever methods we develop, however, will have to preserve the basic character of consciousness.

LIPPMANN: Basic character?

JAMES: Yes, there are at least five integral features of experience that define it as a unique entity.

LIPPMANN: Such as . . . ?

JAMES: Any experience is personal. It's my experience and I understand it in a way that cannot be fully conveyed to others.

LIPPMANN: Is that so? Earlier you described your experience of the red bird in the tree. Your description seemed adequate to me. What was missing?

JAMES: What was missing? The simple fact that you are not me and therefore you can never fully appreciate my experience of the bird in the tree. Sure, I can tell you that I think the bird is pretty. That it reminds me of ones I saw as a youth in Rhode Island. How I struggled to draw them to my satisfaction when I was practicing landscapes. But none of that will arouse in you exactly the same feelings . . . the same *experience* that I have as those memories and associations flood my awareness.

LIPPMANN: Because everyone's past is different, the way that they interpret the present moment will be different.

JAMES: Yes. But it's not just the past—its future goals and aspirations, momentary wants and desires—all these internal states make each experience not just different, but private ... very private. The best I can do is to give you a rough verbal account, but it never fully captures the totality of what I'm experiencing.

LIPPMANN: Alright ... that's the personal nature of consciousness ... you said there were other essential features.

JAMES: Yes. Consciousness is also continuous, like a flowing stream. It's an odd paradox because as I move from one thought to another, each seems discrete, separate from the other. First, I'm thinking about how to describe consciousness to you, then I'm thinking about the redness of the bird, next I'm thinking about painting in Rhode Island, and yet despite the seemingly distinct, detached nature of each of these thoughts, their movement in my mind from one to the other feels smooth and natural.

LIPPMANN: Therefore, any attempt to reduce or atomize this stream of thought to fundamental particulars will lose that essential continuity.

JAMES: Correct. Reduce it and you've lost it. It's not conscious experience anymore.

LIPPMANN: If this stream of thought is ever flowing, then that would suggest that is it highly variable as well ... constantly changing.

JAMES: Indeed ... constantly. Even if you force your mind to hold fast to a single idea, that idea will shift and ooze about in your awareness. So even if I fix myself upon the red bird, my mind strays all about it ... first on its beauty, then its awkward perch, next on how odd it is that Alice finds birdsong more annoying than pleasant ... and so forth. The mind can't help but wander.

LIPPMANN: And as your mind fixes upon the bird, then other aspects of consciousness must be pushed to background.

JAMES: Yes. The allocation of attention over the flowing stream is another essential aspect of our conscious experience. We select out certain elements, pulling them from the stream, so to speak, interpreting them, categorizing them, and associating them with other elements either from the senses or from memory.

LIPPMANN: Surely this process of allocating attention is not random—we don't pay attention to just anything that happens to be in the stream.

JAMES: The mind is a functional, goal-directed instrument. While there may be some things that have a reflexive pull on our attention, such as our name or a threatening screech, generally, we attentionally segment the stream based on our immediate goals. I picked out the red bird not just for its beauty but for its usefulness in our conversation.

LIPPMANN: I see. So ... it is these aspects of consciousness—its personal nature, its continuous flow, its variability and goal directedness—that convince you that any reductionist approach to studying it will prove useless.

JAMES: Oh . . . yes, but there's a final, even more mysterious quality of consciousness; one that seems almost impossible to capture scientifically.

LIPPMANN: What do you mean?

JAMES: Every thought we have, every object we observe, memory we ponder, or idea we twist about in our heads is experienced as being distinct from us and our conscious awareness. They are *in* us . . . *in* our minds . . . but experienced as separate from us and our minds.

LIPPMANN: If I understand you correctly, you're saying that whatever we experience—a thought, a percept—it is internal to us, yet not experienced as being part of us. It is instead distinct from us and our awareness.

JAMES: Yes. It's odd. Even our language reflects this; we don't say, "I'm thinking Fred," we say, "I'm thinking *of* Fred." As if the thought of Fred is an object distinct from us and the thinking process. I don't see how objective methods of study can capture this deeply subjective aspect of experience.

LIPPMANN: What about the idea of *me*?

JAMES: Of me? What do you mean?

LIPPMANN: Well . . . just as I have thoughts about objects I observe or ideas I ponder, I also have the subjective feeling that *I* am the one doing the observing or the pondering. In the stream of thought, there must also be some idea of *me* . . . of myself as the thinking agent.

JAMES: Yes . . . and once again, this points to the deep mystery of how consciousness operates. The idea of the red bird and all the associations that it arouses are thoughts in my stream of consciousness, but the feeling that I am the one doing the observing and thinking must also be a thought, and yet this thought has a very different feel to it. It is not distinct or separate from me as are the others but is instead . . . *me*.

LIPPMANN: What accounts for this distinction?

JAMES: I think the concept of the self as an active, observing, thinking agent must arise from how the body interacts with the world around it. There must be some *organizing framework* that provides a coherent relational context for attended-to aspects of the stream.

LIPPMANN: Organizing framework . . . ? I'm not sure . . .

JAMES: Well . . . there would be a physical aspect to it—the location of the body in space, how the body moves through that space . . . the particulars of how the eyes, ears, and skin interact with the energies of the environment—all of this creates a unique framework from which the stream of sensory inputs is processed and understood.

LIPPMANN: But there's more than just that, I suspect.

JAMES: There would also be a conceptional aspect—how one's past experience, memories, goals, desires, and such affect the allocation of attention across the stream of thought and how one interprets those selected aspects.

LIPPMANN: So this physical and conceptual framework that comprises the "me" of experience . . . it must also be a thought—correct?

JAMES: Yes. It would have to be. But a unique kind of thought that provides the continuity . . . the consistent, coherent reference point from which we understand things. It's a thought that might be expressed as: "I, the active, physical agent called William with this particular identity, past history, future goals, etc. . . . I'm the one observing these objects and pondering these thoughts."

LIPPMANN: So if we put all this together, we have a constant flowing stream of thought . . .

JAMES: . . . Which an organizing framework, that I identify with myself . . .

LIPPMANN: . . . . actively segregates into attended and nonattended aspects . . .

JAMES: . . . based on the wants, goals, and priorities that are foremost at the time.

LIPPMANN: The fact that we have to "carve out" certain aspects of the stream indicates that there is always more information in the stream than can be processed at any given moment.

JAMES: Most definitely. You can't attend to everything. But each thing you attend to always seems to suggest more. There's a rich, extra much-ness that you get with each neatly identified thought.

LIPPMANN: Extra much-ness . . . ?

JAMES: Sure. Think about when I noticed that bird. Immediately, other associated ideas and memories were flooding into my head . . . thoughts about nature, about nature's beauty, about other similar birds, about migration, about my puzzlement over Alice's disliking of birdsong. Every thought has thick, fuzzy boundaries . . . or entanglements with other thoughts and feelings. We must actively inhibit our mental wonderings, or we'd never get anything accomplished.

LIPPMANN: So segregating, interpreting, and inhibiting are essential to making sense out of the stream of thought.

JAMES: Yes, absolutely necessary. The mind that fails to do this successfully is prone to becoming pathological. But as necessary as this is, it also limits and constrains the knowledge that we can acquire from the stream.

LIPPMANN: Limits and constrains . . . you mean we're cutting something out every time we pay attention to one thing rather than another.

JAMES: Yes. Our understanding of the stream is always incomplete—remember that extra much-ness I referred to—a good deal of it is lost whenever we impose a meaningful interpretation on items in the stream.

LIPPMANN: So to interpret something is to give it meaning, which is essential to understanding it, but it also limits it somehow . . .

JAMES: To interpret something one way necessarily strips from it other possible interpretations or meanings—and therefore memories or associations connected to those other meanings.

LIPPMANN: For example . . . ?

JAMES: Suppose I hear a musical chord floating about my stream of thought. I focus my attention on the chord and label it—a D minor chord, often used by Mozart to presage impending doom. The "Mozart D minor," I call it.

LIPPMANN: You have a well-trained musical ear.

JAMES: It's hypothetical . . .

LIPPMANN: So how does that interpretive label limit the experience?

JAMES: The label immediately biases my experience. I'm fond of Mozart, so I react positively to the use of the chord. I may even think, "Modern composers should use that more often," as my body shudders with the sense of tragedy the chord imparts. But this reaction is certainly not the only, or even the best way to experience the chord—but it's *my* way . . . my peculiar, limited, idiosyncratic way of experiencing music. Other composers may have used that same chord to convey very different meanings or feelings—all ignored when I slap the "Mozart D minor" label on it.

LIPPMANN: But since interpretation or categorization is integral to understanding, we have no choice but to impose limits on experience.

JAMES: Correct.

LIPPMANN: Is there any way to recover the meaning that is lost when we categorize sensory inputs?

JAMES: I'm not sure we can entirely recover it, but we can get a vague sense of the true richness of experience before we chop and dissect it into neat and discrete conceptual units.

LIPPMANN: A vague sense . . . ?

JAMES: Yes, I believe there's a form of experience that is preconceptual. Experiences that we occasionally have where we simply let the experience happen without imposing labels or categories on it. Something I refer to as *pure experience*.

LIPPMANN: Pure experience?

JAMES: It may be what the world is like for prelinguistic children. Adults may only experience it under extreme fatigue, anesthesia, or altered or mystical states.

LIPPMANN: If a pure experience is so rare, and something that we apparently outgrow, is there any value to it?

JAMES: I think it tells us that there is more to reality than what our concepts and linguistic labels can capture.

LIPPMANN: More?

JAMES: Our conceptual interpretation of experience . . . the distinctions we impose on it so that it makes sense to us . . . there's an artificiality to this. I'm not saying it's wrong . . . but it's incomplete and too often we are blind to its incompleteness.

LIPPMANN: So what would a more complete understanding of reality tell us?

JAMES: What do mystics tell us?

LIPPMANN: That there's some manner of . . . cosmic unity to all things. That we are part of some larger, grander whole . . .

JAMES: Yes . . . when you transcend logic and reason, you are sometimes overwhelmed by an intuitive sense of infinite unity. The self-object distinction . . . the "me separate from you or it" . . . somehow this is lost, and we come to understand the self as . . . not so much a discrete *thing* but a *process* of becoming more related to the world around us.

LIPPMANN: That doesn't entirely make sense.

JAMES: No, it doesn't . . . because it's an intuitive feel, not a logical proposition. But it's one that for many people appears to enhance the quality of their lives.

LIPPMANN: And maybe in the end, that's the most important thing. After all, what could be more important than the quality of life lived?

JAMES: Nothing . . . Mr. Lippmann. Nothing at all.

They reach the front gate of James's house. James gives Lippmann an approving nod.

JAMES: You're a promising student, Mr. Lippmann.

LIPPMANN: Thank you, sir.

Chapter 3

Why So Radical?[1]

Topic: Radical empiricism

Student: Mary Whiton Calkins

Outline:

Defining Empirical
   Empirical versus rational
   Identifying the origin of experience
   The unity of experience
Experience as the fundamental substance of the universe
Taking experience seriously
   The failure of philosophy
   The experience of rationality
   Tough-minded versus tender-minded personalities
Radical empirical approach to philosophy

Mary Whiton Calkins

Mary Whiton Calkins was born on March 30, 1863, in Hartford, Connecticut. In 1884, she graduated from Smith College. After graduating, she took a job teaching Greek at Wellesley College. Wellesley asked Calkins to consider teaching classes in the emerging field of psychology. Hearing of Calkin's interest in psychology, William James invited her to sit in on his lectures at Harvard. When male students boycotted James's classes because of her presence, James tutored her privately. In 1892, she was formally admitted as a "guest" at Harvard because the university did not, at that time, admit women as students. In 1895, she completed her thesis work in psychology. However, despite unanimous

---

[1] Based largely on the following Jamesian essays: "The meaning of truth" (especially the preface)," "The sentiment of rationality," "Does consciousness exist," "The place of affectional facts in a world of pure experience," and "The pragmatist account of truth and its misunderstanders," from the *Philosophical Review, 17* (January 1908), p. 1.

approval from her committee (which included James), she was denied an official degree. She returned to Wellesley, where she had a long and distinguished career as both a psychologist and philosopher. She served as the first female president of the American Psychological Association and the American Philosophical Association.

James scans the late autumn sky of Cambridge, Massachusetts. It is a bright, beautiful afternoon but with an unmistakable chill of impending winter in the air. As he reaches into his breast pocket for his pipe, he notices a solitary student, Mary Whiton Calkins, sitting on the grass quietly reading. He approaches.

JAMES: Miss Calkins.

CALKINS: (looking up to see James approaching) Oh . . . yes, Professor James . . .

JAMES: Is that . . . Schopenhauer you're reading?

CALKINS: Yes. For my philosophy seminar.

JAMES: Gloomy old fellow.

CALKINS: Yes, but his arguments are not without merit, I think.

JAMES: Agreed. He must be taken seriously. But does his pessimism follow from his philosophy, or does he philosophize to justify his pessimism?

CALKINS: (caught off guard by the question) . . . ahh, I'm not entirely sure. I hadn't thought about it that way . . .

JAMES: (smiling) Of no consequence . . . a discussion for another time.

CALKINS: (a bit confused) Okay . . .

JAMES: No, I disturbed you because I wanted to remind you that you still owe me a paper from our previous sessions.

CALKINS: Oh, yes. I've been working on that. I should be able to complete it this evening.

JAMES: Well then, I won't keep you. I'll expect it in the morning.

James nods farewell to Calkins and departs down Oxford Street toward his home. Before he gets very far, however, she catches him from behind.

CALKINS: Ahh . . . well, Professor James, actually . . . .

James turns.

JAMES: Yes?

CALKINS: Umm . . . about that paper . . .

JAMES: Yes . . . ?

CALKINS: . . . The reason it's been delayed . . . you see . . .

JAMES: No need to explain. I understand your situation is rather unique . . .

CALKINS: Well, in this case, it's not so much the challenges of my situation that delayed me but my understanding of the topic. I've been struggling with that somewhat . . .

JAMES: I see. So what's the nature of your struggle?

CALKINS: I'd say . . . it's the whole topic.

JAMES: The whole topic?

CALKINS: Yes.

JAMES: Well, forgive an old professor, but it's been a while . . . what exactly was your topic?

CALKINS: Your notion of radical empiricism.

JAMES: Radical empiricism?

CALKINS: Yes, I was going to summarize the main points.

JAMES: I see . . .

CALKINS: But I got stuck right at the start.

JAMES: . . . Right at the start . . .

CALKINS: Yes. I'm having trouble grasping the . . . *radical* part.

JAMES: What's so radical about radical empiricism—is that the idea?

CALKINS: Precisely.

JAMES: Well, Miss Calkins, let's begin . . . (a sudden gust of wind nearly takes James's hat off; he reflexively slaps his hand down on his head to hold it in place) . . . Whoa!

CALKINS: Nearly lost your hat, sir!

JAMES: Yes . . . (James notices clouds gathering far off in the distance) I wonder if inclement weather is on the way.

CALKINS: This time of year, it's not uncommon.

JAMES: Indeed. Now where were we?

CALKINS: Uhh . . . the radical part of radical empiricism.

JAMES: Right. Well . . . the place to begin is with the idea of empiricism itself. What can you tell me about that?

CALKINS: That was the idea . . . about the importance of experience in shaping the human mind—correct? Mill . . . Hume—all those British philosophers who thought that the environment wrote upon the blank slate of the human mind.

JAMES: Alright. Good enough start. So . . . empirical for them referred to observational experience. Taking in environmental events and information and learning from them.

CALKINS: Right . . . yes. I recall that from our discussions.

JAMES: And do you recall some of the criticisms of that approach?

CALKINS: Well . . . the blank slate idea . . . didn't some others argue we shouldn't . . . well . . . that it is . . . oversimplified to regard the mind as just . . . lying there . . .

JAMES: Okay . . . yes. Some argued that if taken to an extreme, the Empiricists' view led to the notion that the mind was simply a passive organ . . . that it contributed nothing to its own development. An idea that seemed at odds with the active, exploratory behavior of infants and children.

CALKINS: Too extreme . . . right, so that's the radical part of radical empiricism—right? You're a radical empiricist if you regard the mind as passive.

JAMES: Some might say that, but that's not what I mean when I refer to radical empiricism.

CALKINS: (rather deflated) Oh, I see.

JAMES: Let's try this—pretend for a moment that you are John Mill or David Hume, one of those pesky British Empiricists. Give me an example of an *empirical* experience.

CALKINS: Well . . . how about a young child putting his hand too close to an oil lamp and getting a burn. From that, the child quickly learns to avoid fire for fear of pain.

JAMES: Okay . . . a simple enough example. Now let me ask you a question.

CALKINS: Okay.

JAMES: What was the *empirical* part of that experience?

CALKINS: The empirical part . . . ? I'm not sure what you mean.

JAMES: Well, if you were Hume or Mill . . . what part of that experience would you say was the most important for learning to avoid fire?

CALKINS: Oh . . . well, I guess I'd say the heat of the flame.

JAMES: Okay, so the heat of the flame causes the child discomfort and from this, the child learns to avoid fire.

CALKINS: Yes, that all sounds correct.

JAMES: And the specifically *empirical* part of this experience is what happened *externally*—the heat from the lamp's flame. In other words, to be empirical is to be *outside of* or *external to* the mind that is doing the learning.

CALKINS: Yes, right. If I recall correctly, didn't we define empirical as "whatever is verified by observation or experience?"

JAMES: That's the traditional understanding of the word.

CALKINS: So what we're observing or experiencing is always *out there* (she gestures toward the external environment)—right?

JAMES: Traditionally a dichotomy has been assumed between empirical and rational. Empirical is based on external observation or experience. Rational is based on internal processes such as logic or imagery. This goes all the way back to Plato and Aristotle. But the dichotomy is a false one. It doesn't exist.

CALKINS: A false dichotomy?

JAMES: Yes. Very much so. Let's look more closely at the example you gave.

CALKINS: Okay . . . ?

JAMES: You told me the heat from the flame led to discomfort for the child and from that he learned to avoid fire.

CALKINS: Right.

JAMES: And the flame's heat is *external* to the child's mind. That makes it *empirical*. It's coming from out there (James gestures out into the environment) and affects the mind in here (pointing to his head).

CALKINS: Correct.

JAMES: No, wrong.

CALKINS: Oh . . . ?

JAMES: If you think about it, it's not the flame of the lamp—that thing outside of the child's body—that's leading to fear of the fire. It's the discomfort the child experiences.

CALKINS: Well . . . yes . . . I suppose, technically, that is true.

JAMES: If we could have protected the child's hand in some way so that the flame's heat did not affect it, then the child would have learned nothing—correct?

CALKINS: Yes. I suppose so.

JAMES: So it's not what happened *out there* (pointing to the external world) that produced the learning, it was what happened *in here* (pointing at his head).

CALKINS: Okay. I see that. It makes sense, I suppose.

JAMES: In fact, you can't even say that the heat of the flame was something external to the child.

CALKINS: Really? You can't? What do you mean?

JAMES: The lamp, the flame, the heat . . . these were all percepts in the child's mind. The entire experience—the flame . . . the discomfort . . . what was seen . . . what was felt . . . the reaction of withdrawing the hand . . . it all happened *in here* (pointing to the head) . . . none of it was *out there* (pointing to the world).

CALKINS: But . . . something about that doesn't make sense . . .

JAMES: What . . . ?

CALKINS: Well . . . it seems to me that there wouldn't have been anything happening here (points to her head) if there hadn't been something out there (points to the world). So can't we say that experience requires some external signal to . . . get going in the first place.

JAMES: So for you to have any experience happening up here (points to the head) you first must have some signal originating out there (points to the world). Is that what you're saying?

CALKINS: Right.

JAMES: Close your eyes and think of grandma and the wonderful meals she would make at those family feasts.

CALKINS: What?

JAMES: I'm serious. Do it. Close your eyes and think of grandma. Or think of something . . . *anything* that is emotionally significant for you.

CALKINS: Oh . . . I see.

The two pause their walk as Calkins closes her eyes.

CALKINS: Well . . . I'm thinking of the hiking trip I took with some friends when I was in Greece. On the way up the trail, I smashed my toe rather badly on a rock, but I didn't want to spoil things for everyone, so I pretended it was nothing and kept climbing. Andres was my friend's snotty little brother who kept saying rich

Americans were too soft to make it all the way up the hill. So I made sure I beat him to the top, but by then my toe was throbbing. It took all my strength to hold back the tears. Still, it was exhilarating, and the view of the olive orchards below was unforgettable.

JAMES: What are you having right now?

CALKINS: (opening her eyes) What am I having right now? I'm not sure what you mean.

JAMES: Close your eyes! Keep thinking about Greece, your throbbing toe, snotty little Andres, the olive orchards . . . all that, keep thinking about it.

CALKINS: Okay.

JAMES: What are you having right now?

CALKINS: (cautiously) . . . An experience . . . ?

JAMES: Most assuredly! And this is what the old British Empiricists and others failed to appreciate. They fell into the same false dichotomy as earlier philosophers. They wanted to carve up experience into the empirical part—what your senses are telling you about the world out there, and the rational part—what goes on inside your head . . . your mental calculations . . . your imaginings and fantasies. But experience is *one* thing. There's no empirical type of experience contrasted with a rational type. All of it is experience.

CALKINS: One thing? But how is that possible? Surely I have to separate my imaginings from my perceptions, otherwise I'm prone to madness, aren't I?

JAMES: Every aspect of our experience has a relationship to other aspects, and we can use those relationships to help us identify the origin of the experience.

CALKINS: The origin . . . meaning whether it's internally generated or a sensory signal—correct?

JAMES: Yes.

CALKINS: So how do relationships to other aspects of experience allow us to identify its source?

JAMES: An internal signal's relationships are different than an external signal.

CALKINS: How so?

JAMES: Both an imagined fire and an observed one may arouse memories of youthful camping trips. But with an imagined fire, I will not experience a warming of the body as I would with an observed fire.

CALKINS: So that "warming of the body" experience is one of the ways I can tell that the fire is resulting from sensory input rather than my imagination.

JAMES: Correct. When you observe a fire, you'll also experience your body warming up. When you imagine a fire, you won't.

CALKINS: And what might an imagined fire be related to that an observed fire would not?

JAMES: My house.

CALKINS: What?

JAMES: My house. I could imagine my house burning down, but, hopefully, I will never observe it.

CALKINS: I see . . .

JAMES: The critical point is that all of this—the imagined fire, the observed fire, the warming of the body, my house—these are all aspects of *one thing*: experience, and the relationships among these aspects are informing us about the source of the experience—from the senses or from the mind.

CALKINS: I see . . .

JAMES: Furthermore, identifying the likely source of an experience is only one of many things we do using the network of relations among aspects of experience.

CALKINS: What are some of the other things?

JAMES: Formulating an emotional reaction to it—do I approach or avoid? Interpreting the meaning of it—is it helpful or harmful to my goals and desires? Adjusting our motor actions relative to it—should I grip it firmly or use a light touch? Honestly, I have a hard time thinking of anything we do with an experience that does not entail some understanding of how that experience is related to others. Why do we so stubbornly fixate on its origin?

CALKINS: I suppose because whether an experience originates from within or without plays a defining role in how we construct reality. If it's "out there" (pointing to the environment), then it's real. If its "in here" (pointing to his head), then it's just imagination . . . just a mental construction.

JAMES: But that's the fundamental point I'm trying to make—it's *all* mental construction based on relationships, regardless of origin.

CALKINS: But isn't there an objective reality associated with sensory inputs that is not present with our memories or imaginings?

JAMES: Ahh . . . I love that word *objective*, Miss Calkins. It has such an authoritative timbre. If it's objective, it's real, it's substantial, it's . . . scientific. But what you and my many skeptical colleagues don't seem to grasp is that whatever it is we label *objective*, we do it *subjectively* (a long slow sigh). Look, you just had a vivid experience of hiking in Greece with your friends—correct?

CALKINS: Yes, but it was based on what I recalled from memory, not from actually being in Greece.

JAMES: Allow me to shake your faith in sensory inputs as the unfettered source of what is real.

CALKINS: Shake at will, Professor James.

JAMES: What convinced you that it was from memory and not because you were actually in Greece?

CALKINS: (a modest laugh) Well . . . because I'm seeing the generally flat autumn landscape of Cambridge before my eyes and not the rugged Greek hills.

JAMES: Do you dream at night, Miss Calkins?

CALKINS: (shrugging her shoulders) Of course. Doesn't everyone?

JAMES: Pretty much so, I think. Ever have a dream that you were back on that Greek hiking trail?

CALKINS: Sure.

JAMES: Odd thing about dreams . . . they're so convincingly real when we have them. I bet you felt as if you were really there on that stony trail, Andres goading you on while your toe was pounding in agony.

CALKINS: Yes, dreams feel real when you're having one.

JAMES: All of that happening, despite the fact that your eyes were seeing the inside of your eyelids, not the rugged Greek hills.

CALKINS: Okay . . . so I'm not entirely sure what that example demonstrates . . .

JAMES: You told me that it was sensory inputs that convinced you that you were not having a *real* experience. You *imagined* you were back in Greece, and you knew it was imagination because your eyes were telling you that you were in Cambridge.

CALKINS: Right.

JAMES: But I just showed you that every night you have real experiences that are completely at odds with your sensory inputs. Reality is what we construct in our heads, not necessarily what sensory inputs tell us.

CALKINS: But is it fair to use dreams to support that argument? Isn't the sleeping state . . . a rather mysterious anomaly?

JAMES: Maybe . . . ? If you'd be more convinced by a waking example, then consider this: A man falls asleep in his bedroom as he has done night after night for decades.

CALKINS: He's of sound mind . . . sober . . . no maladies of note?

JAMES: Absolutely . . . in the prime of both physical and mental health.

CALKINS: Okay . . . ?

JAMES: Now do you recall some time ago when we discussed Mr. Wheatstone's invention—the stereoscope?

CALKINS: Yes, that neat little device that gives one highly realistic visual impressions.

JAMES: Right, you look into it and see a photograph, but the lenses are adjusted such that you get a compelling sense of three dimensionality.

CALKINS: Yes, almost as if you're *in* the photograph. About as close to actually being there as you can get.

JAMES: Imagine we've created a set of stereoscopic goggles, so light that you can't even sense when you're wearing them.

CALKINS: Alright.

JAMES: Now here's our diabolical little plan. Into our stereoscopic goggles, we put a photograph of the dinosaur room of the London Natural History Museum. We wait until our gentleman sleeper is off into a deep, deep slumber and surreptitiously put the goggles on him. When he awakens, where will he think he is?

CALKINS: Well . . . I imagine that we're going to put him in an extraordinary state of confusion.

JAMES: A reasonable conjecture. But . . . where will he think he is?

CALKINS: Normally, when we awaken, we immediately recall where we fell asleep the night before, and you said he's been sleeping in the same bedroom for decades.

JAMES: Correct.

CALKINS: So he would have every expectation of arising in his own bedroom.

JAMES: But what are his senses telling him?

CALKINS: That he's in the dinosaur room of the London Natural History Museum.

JAMES: Does his physical location . . . his *objective reality* . . . better correspond to what his senses are telling him or what his memory informs him of?

CALKINS: In this case, he'd do better to trust his memory.

JAMES: You told me earlier that you knew were in Cambridge because of what your senses were telling you. You trusted them, and not your memory, to give you an accurate read on reality.

CALKINS: Right.

JAMES: But our recently roused sleeper had better do the opposite.

CALKINS: So sometimes reality is what my senses tell me and sometimes reality has little or nothing to do with sensory inputs—is that what you're saying?

JAMES: Hmm . . . . close but not exactly. Reality is what you experience, and your experience is a combination of sensory inputs, memories, expectations, goals, and desires—all combined into one thing in your head.

CALKINS: So there's no empirical experience versus rational experience. There's only experience, and we engage with *all* experience the same way—by relating aspects of our experience with other aspects in order to understand it.

JAMES: Correct.

CALKINS: So is this what is radical about radical empiricism?

JAMES: Yes. That's the first part of it. It's radical because I reject any important distinction between empirical and rational. Both are merely aspects of one thing called experience, and to understand experience we relate certain aspects of experience to other aspects.

CALKINS: Okay, I think I've got that. But you said that's only the first part of what makes radical empiricism, radical.

JAMES: Yes. The radical part goes even deeper.

CALKINS: How so?

JAMES: This one thing that we call experience turns out to be the fundamental substance of the universe.

CALKINS: Fundamental substance of the universe . . . ?

JAMES: Correct. Some of my colleagues will tell you that fundamentally the universe comes down to matter. Others will tell you that ultimately the universe is some sort of grand unified consciousness. But I think both are badly mistaken.

CALKINS: Is that so? Mistaken how?

JAMES: Both reduce the universe to something utterly inconsequential.

CALKINS: Inconsequential?

JAMES: Yes. Of what consequence is unexperienced matter? If matter just floats around and nothing or nobody knows it's there, then it might as well not exist at all. For matter, to *matter* it must be experienced.

CALKINS: And consciousness—how can it be inconsequential?

JAMES: Because a consciousness that does not experience anything is empty. Of what use is an empty consciousness. No . . . fundamentally for the universe to exist at all, there must be experience. Without it, nothing else is of any value.

CALKINS: I see.

JAMES: Ultimately, if the universe comes down to experience, then there is a truth in experience that must be taken seriously. Radical empiricism means that we take experience, *all* experience, seriously.

CALKINS: You mean that we haven't been taking experience seriously?

JAMES: Not seriously enough. We've contented ourselves with the notion that we can value some kinds of experience over others. Scientific experience . . . ahhh . . . that's by far the best. That tells us the unvarnished truth, while other forms of experience are inferior . . . even delusional.

CALKINS: But hasn't the progress we've made using science proven its worth?

JAMES: Yes . . . its worth in revealing reliable cause-effect relations. But it tells us nothing about values . . . about living a good life . . . it provides no wisdom for making difficult choices or judgments.

CALKINS: Well . . . wouldn't those questions be in the domain of philosophy rather than science?

JAMES: Agreed. But what kind of progress has philosophy made over the past two thousand years?

CALKINS: Hasn't it provided rules of logic for deciding if a conclusion is valid or not?

JAMES: If those rules were so effective, then why haven't we agreed on one philosophical system for providing rational, satisfying answers to our deepest questions?

CALKINS: For you that would indicate progress?

JAMES: Science has settled on an effective method for uncovering cause-effect relationships. Why can't philosophers settle on an effective method for providing wisdom? We've had Platonists, Neo-Platonists, Aristotelians, Stoics, Scholastics,

Humanists, Positivists, Empiricists, Absolutists, Idealists . . . on and on through the centuries . . . endlessly combating with one another about what's good or true or beautiful. No end in sight.

CALKINS: And you think this endless combating is because we have not taken experience seriously enough.

JAMES: Unquestionably.

CALKINS: How so?

JAMES: Too often, philosophers get lost in abstractions that have little relevance to how people live their lives.

CALKINS: I'm not sure what you mean.

JAMES: Consider this: Suppose my brother takes a substantial sum of money I loaned him and spends it in what I consider a frivolous way.

CALKINS: I imagine you might not be pleased with that.

JAMES: Indeed. Now I must decide if I should confront him on the issue or stay quiet and trust that he will, in the end, pay me back as promised.

CALKINS: A bit of a dilemma. You could argue for the merit of either course of action.

JAMES: Right. Now in making this decision, is it of any consequence whether the universe is of a single spiritual substance as Hegel argues or is but mindless matter blindly following physical laws as Positivists contend?

CALKINS: Seems that both of those are rather far removed from the issue.

JAMES: Right. And that's how it frequently is with philosophy. Its arguments are up in the clouds rather than down here on earth. That's why for centuries it has made little difference in people's lives.

CALKINS: And the remedy is a more serious appreciation of experience?

JAMES: Yes. This is why I have proposed that the first postulate of radical empiricism should be that the only issues debatable among philosophers are those grounded in experience. Clever, magnificent abstractions that have no hope of ever affecting our experience should play no role in our philosophical discussions.

CALKINS: So if philosophical debates must be grounded in experience, you think that will make philosophy more relevant to real life.

JAMES: Yes. It will force philosophers to recognize that philosophy is an experience, just like anything else in life.

CALKINS: Philosophy is an experience?

JAMES: Experience is *one* thing. It includes philosophy. However, philosophy has worked under the mistaken belief that it is a detached, theoretical . . . *rational* pursuit that, if done properly, generates conclusions that all will recognize as credible.

CALKINS: I see . . .

JAMES: Take the Scholastics, for example . . .

CALKINS: The Scholastics . . . ? You mean the Christian philosophers in Middle Ages who thought that they could use reason to prove the existence of God . . .

JAMES: Yes, yes. They presumed that their arguments, if constructed rigorously enough, would be convincing to all . . . believers and nonbelievers alike. If you had a mind capable of reason, you would be forced to accept the Scholastics' conclusion because . . . reason is reason . . . logical conclusions are simply logical conclusions. They can't be denied.

CALKINS: And what happened?

JAMES: Centuries of debate. Those who already had an inclination toward believing in God found the arguments compelling and those who were inclined not to believe in God found them wanting.

CALKINS: And you would contend that this example is not exceptional but the general pattern.

JAMES: Name your issue . . . free will, consciousness, morality, truth, soul, justice, human purpose . . . has philosophy settled any of these issues? Or have we merely engaged in unending debates, century upon century, with no end in sight?

CALKINS: It seems we're still debating.

JAMES: Indeed. We don't construct rational arguments the way an engineer builds a locomotive. It's not a mechanical process. It's an experience. We *experience* rationality. We *feel* our way through arguments.

CALKINS: We experience rationality? What do you mean? How can we have an experience of something being reasonable?

JAMES: Hmmm . . . let's try an example. Hopefully one close to your heart.

CALKINS: Okay . . . ?

JAMES: Despite my undeniable prowess as a teacher, I'm willing to wager that we've covered a topic or two that you initially found confusing, if not downright indecipherable.

CALKINS: Umm . . . some topics have been challenging. Our present one, for example—radical empiricism—has been somewhat perplexing.

JAMES: And as I droned on and on about this perplexing topic, did you, on occasion, happen to squirm about in your chair while a painful expression wrote itself upon your face?

CALKINS: When you're a classroom of one, it is hard to hide that discomfort you feel when something makes no sense.

JAMES: Ahh . . . yes, *discomfort* you say.

CALKINS: Sure. Confusion leads one to doubt oneself . . . one's intellectual prowess . . . one's prospects for success—it's unquestionably discomforting.

JAMES: Yes. I call that the discomfort of irrationality. You experienced discomfort informing you that you were in the presence of something irrational . . . something that didn't make sense.

CALKINS: And so the inverse would apply as well . . . is that where you're going?

JAMES: Just as we experience the discomfort of irrationality, we experience the relaxing relief . . . the comforting blanket, you might say, of rationality.

CALKINS: That *ahh hah* experience when what were once contradictory pieces seem to fall together into a meaningful pattern.

JAMES: Exactly. We say to ourselves, "Ahh . . . yes. That makes sense. Now I see it." We *experience* reason. We feel it. And this is what philosophers have been doing for centuries. They have been constructing logical arguments that give them an experience of rationality. Arguments that make them feel good.

CALKINS: So Anselm . . . already a committed Christian . . .

JAMES: An archbishop!

CALKINS: Makes himself feel better by constructing what he considers to be a rational argument for God.

JAMES: Sure, but let's not single out the good bishop for special castigation. This is what all philosophers do. They start with the conclusion, which their temperaments and personalities incline them toward, and they build arguments to support that conclusion that give them an experience of rationality. Their seemingly inscrutable logic allows them to smugly say to themselves, "See . . . I was right all along. That should convince my muddle-headed opponents."

CALKINS: And when they confront the arguments of their opponents?

JAMES: They get that uncomfortable experience of irrationality. Their guts tell them, "Nonsense. That simply cannot be right." And they set about constructing a refutation to restore their equilibrium.

CALKINS: (with palpable delight) So . . . does Schopenhauer's pessimism follow from his philosophy, or does he philosophize to justify his pessimism?

JAMES: It seems that discussion for another time has seen its time!

CALKINS: But that's what you're saying—correct? Schopenhauer's pessimism doesn't arise from his philosophy, rather his philosophy arises from his pessimism.

JAMES: Just as surely as Anselm's arises from his faith.

CALKINS: So you believe that centuries of philosophical debate ultimately reduce to clashes of personality?

JAMES: A bit crude, but yes. I think it has been little better than that. Among philosophers you find two broad temperaments, and therefore, philosophies, built around those temperaments.

CALKINS: What kind of temperaments?

JAMES: There are those who are largely optimistic about life, who prefer thinking synthetically, that is, finding commonalities among disparate parts. They have a predilection for developing grand theories or principles. They're more sympathetic toward free will and religious thinking—Hegel and Kant are nice examples. I think of them as tender-minded folks.

CALKINS: And the other?

JAMES: The reverse in character. They tend to be more pessimistic, materialistic, analytical, and reductionistic. They stick closely to empirical facts and look with skepticism on religion and free will. I call them the tough minded—Schopenhauer and Comte are good representatives of this category.

CALKINS: I'm not sure where I'd fit in those categories.

JAMES: I'm sure most of us are a bit of both, but with leanings one way or another. The important point, however, is that temperamental inclinations bias our experience. So it is by temperament that one is likely to accept or reject logical arguments.

CALKINS: So you're saying tough-minded philosophers will simply never accept a tender-minded philosophy and vice-versa.

JAMES: Right. That should be the lesson we take from centuries of ongoing debates and stalemate.

CALKINS: And you think radical empiricism offers a solution to this stalemate?

JAMES: I won't be so bold as to say a solution, but I think it gives us a new way of evaluating philosophical ideas that may aid in getting philosophy out of its rut.

CALKINS: And what is the nature of the "new way of evaluating" philosophical ideas?

JAMES: By our experience with them. Radical empiricism asks, "how does a philosophical proposition stand up to experience?"

CALKINS: For example . . . ?

JAMES: Imagine for a moment buying wholesale into the materialistic view of the universe.

CALKINS: Materialistic view . . . ?

JAMES: That the universe is nothing but mindless matter following physical laws—including us . . . you and me.

CALKINS: Okay . . . ?

James. Do you experience the world as nothing but mindless matter? Do I seem like an automaton fumbling robotically about to you?

CALKINS: No. You seem more like a mindful agent, making his own choices, pursuing his own plans and goals.

JAMES: Try living your life in accordance with any philosophical system that denies human free will. "Oh . . . yes," the materialists and positivists will say, "it certainly seems as if we are free agents. But in reality, it simply cannot be so. Therefore, we should dispense with the illusion and face the truth." Fine! Try it. Try living your life as if you and everyone around you is a fully predetermined piece of machinery and not a human being capable of formulating goals and making choices. Goodness! If I were to implement some philosophical notions, I'd be a street pauper . . . out of work, depended on charity.

CALKINS: What do you mean?

JAMES: Well, good Mr. William Clifford has argued that it is an act of downright immorality to hold any belief in the absence of sufficient evidence. Now I'm sure the Positivists would praise such a commandment, but if I took it seriously, I'd have to find another profession.

CALKINS: Really?

JAMES: Being a teacher requires a daily faith commitment to the ultimate success of one's students despite the vast evidence they display to the contrary.

CALKINS: Oh . . . yes. I imagine we can be frustrating sometimes.

JAMES: Indeed.

CALKINS: So in your estimation, if a philosophical proposition fundamentally counters our experience, the proposition should be abandoned.

JAMES: Yes. It has no utility. If philosophers insist on debating their abstractions for the mere sake of mental exercise, then so be it. But if philosophy is to make a difference in how people live their lives . . . if it is to offer wisdom for living a better life, then it needs to remain grounded in experience. That's the great lesson of radical empiricism.

CALKINS: So if I understand you correctly, to be a radical empiricist one must accept that experience is a unified entity. The traditional empirical/rational distinction is false.

JAMES: Correct.

CALKINS: Furthermore, experience is the fundamental substance of universe, containing within it a truth that must be taken seriously by all—especially philosophers.

JAMES: Do you think that is enough to complete your paper?

CALKINS: I'm sure I'll be writing late into the night, but you'll have it in the morning.

JAMES: I look forward to reading it. Good evening, Miss Calkins.

CALKINS: Good evening, Professor James.

Chapter 4

A Universe of Many[1]

Topic: Pluralism

Student: George Santayana

Outline:

Does pluralism mean fragmentation?
Pluralism versus monism
   Idealism/dialectical monism
   Materialism
   Consciousness/the experience of knowing
   Dualism
Pure experience and the emergence of plentitude
The never, not quite of experience
Interconnected plurality
The essentiality of community
Culture and the role of the individual

George Santayana

George Santayana was born in 1863 in Madrid, Spain, and moved to Boston in 1872. He attended Harvard from 1882 to 1889, where he earned both a BA and a PhD. The year of his graduation also marked the start of his service on the Harvard faculty. Thus, he was both a student and colleague of William James. Santayana was a central figure in what has become known as Classical American Philosophy, while also being a prolific literary critic and poet. He authored dozens of books on philosophy, history, literature, and poetry. He is also well known for his quips and

---

[1] This chapter owes much to Goodman, R. B. (2012). William James's pluralisms. *International Review of Philosophy, 2*, 155–76. Also, James's essays "On a certain blindness in human beings" in *Talks to teachers on psychology and to students on some of life's Ideals* (New York: Henry Holt, 1899) and "The importance of individuals." Also, James's book *A pluralistic universe.*

aphorisms such as, "those who cannot remember the past are doomed to repeat it" and "only the dead have seen the end of war." He also appears to be one of James's few associates who had a less than warm relationship with him.

George Santayana waits pensively in the Harvard quad for William James to exit the lecture hall. James emerges, perches his hat upon his head, and begins a relaxed stroll home.

SANTAYANA: Professor James.

James turns to see Santayana approaching.

JAMES: Ahh . . . Mr. Santayana. How are you this fine afternoon?

SANTAYANA: Very well, sir . . . and you?

JAMES: Excellent.

SANTAYANA: I wonder if I might pose some questions regarding your last lecture.

JAMES: Of course. Always happy to weed out any confusions I might have sown.

SANTAYANA: Yes . . . well . . . I did have some confusion . . . some . . . rather serious concerns, actually.

JAMES: Serious concerns . . . ? Well, we'd better clear things up. I'd hate to cause you unnecessary mental distress.

SANTAYANA: Thank you. I appreciate that.

James pauses and plants a thoughtful gaze at Santayana.

JAMES: Mr. Santayana, you impress me as a young man of sober disposition. I hope you dedicate some time to leisure . . . recreation . . . lighter fare of sorts.

SANTAYANA: Oh . . . yes . . . occasionally, I guess.

JAMES: That's important, you know. One should guard against becoming too dour about life, especially in one's youth.

SANTAYANA: I'll try to keep that in mind.

JAMES: Good . . . now . . . Oxford Street or Divinity Avenue?

SANTAYANA: Sir?

JAMES: Well, I'm on my way home. I'm famished. With any good luck, Alice will have dinner waiting.

SANTAYANA: I see . . . .

JAMES: So I can take Oxford Street or Divinity Avenue, either one takes me to Irving. Do you have a preference?

SANTAYANA: Oh . . . either is fine for me as well.

JAMES: Oxford it is.

SANTAYANA: I've been thinking through some of the ideas you presented in class . . .

JAMES: Good. Glad to hear that my lectures stimulate thought.

SANTAYANA: Well . . . forgive me if I sound blunt, but . . .

JAMES: No worries, Mr. Santayana, I appreciate candor, and in the academic business one quickly grows a thick skin.

SANTAYANA: It seems to me that some of your ideas are . . . well . . . shall I say, pessimistic at best and . . .

JAMES: . . . at worst . . . ?

SANTAYANA: . . . I'd say . . . divisive and maybe even dangerous.

JAMES: Really . . . ? Well . . . that's certainly not my intention, but sometimes we may not recognize the ramifications of what we propose. What specifically are you referring to?

SANTAYANA: It was your discussion the other day of pluralism . . . and the idea of a pluralistic universe . . .

JAMES: Pluralism . . . dangerous . . . ? I'm surprised. I've always considered the idea just the opposite. I think of it as a way of respecting differences and creating greater tolerance.

SANTAYANA: Yes, I remember you mentioning that in class, but I fear there may be some implications of it that you're not considering.

JAMES: Oh . . . ? Implications . . . such as . . . ?

SANTAYANA: Well . . . if creating unity is an impossibility, then aren't you giving people license to indulge in their prejudices and . . .

JAMES: Wait . . . wait . . . I don't believe I ever said that pluralism excludes any possibility of unity . . .

SANTAYANA: But if there's no common concept or substance that pervades the universe, then isn't striving for some manner of integration merely wasted effort?

JAMES: No, I don't think so. But . . . I'm concerned that your understanding of what I mean by pluralism is . . . well . . . incomplete at best and . . .

SANTAYANA: . . . At worst . . .

JAMES: . . . In need of serious repair, shall we say.

SANTAYANA: Repair . . . ?

JAMES: Yes. Let's start here: What do you think I mean by pluralism?

SANTAYANA: Well . . . that fundamentally the universe is . . . fragmented . . . composed of a multitude of unique parts or aspects that cannot be reduced to a common substance or concept.

JAMES: Alright . . . a fair enough starting point. Yes, pluralism is to be contrasted with monism. Monism says that ultimately the universe is some kind of great big *One*—one substance . . . one mind . . . one grand overarching concept from which everything else emanates.

SANTAYANA: . . . And pluralism disputes this claiming that the universe is instead a collection of many . . .

JAMES: Correct . . . many substances or many minds or concepts.

SANTAYANA: And that these many things cannot be brought together in any way and therefore . . .

JAMES: No . . . not exactly. Pluralism is not saying that these many substances or minds cannot be interconnect in some way . . . but let's not get too far ahead of ourselves.

SANTAYANA: Okay . . . ?

JAMES: Do you understand why I find pluralism a superior model of the universe compared to various forms of monism?

SANTAYANA: Because we *experience* the universe as a multiplicity of things and not as a single thing.

JAMES: (a modest chuckle) Well, Mr. Santayana, if nothing else you have learned that making reference to experience will always elicit a positive response on my part. Yes, that is true. Our experience of the world is a pluralistic one, not monistic in any sense. But we need to go further and explore why that experience of pluralism is important.

SANTAYANA: Okay.

JAMES: Let us first take up the case of our adversaries—those who boldly pronounce that "our experience be damned!" Whether we like it or not . . . or whether we *experience* it or not . . . the truth of monism simply cannot be denied.

SANTAYANA: And who are our adversaries?

JAMES: They are legion. We find ourselves besieged on all sides, I'm afraid. On our left flank are the rationalists and idealists—those who claim the universe ultimately reduces to a single great mind or thought.

SANTAYANA: And what compels them to make such a claim?

JAMES: Well . . . of late Hegel and his dialectical approach have invigorated idealistic thinking.

SANTAYANA: Dialectic . . . doesn't that go all the back to Socrates?

JAMES: Yes, the general paradigm is the same. A proposition is put forth. Counterarguments are made, and a new broader proposition emerges.

SANTAYANA: Such as . . . ?

JAMES: Suppose someone claims that justice should be understood as "everyone getting what they deserve."

SANTAYANA: Seems reasonable enough.

JAMES: Maybe so, but another might raise a scenario that challenges this. For example, suppose that I recently borrowed a sword from my friend. He deserves to have it returned. But what if in the interim my friend has become mentally unstable and is almost certain to harm someone with the sword. Is it unjust to withhold the sword from him?

SANTAYANA: Ahh . . . yes. I see. That definition is inadequate in situations where innocent people might be harmed by following it.

JAMES: Correct. So we need to modify our definition. How about "justice is all *responsible citizens* getting what they deserve"?

SANTAYANA: Uh huh . . . I see . . . by virtue of his mental instability, my friend no longer qualifies as a "responsible citizen," thus under this definition he may not necessarily be given what he deserves.

JAMES: Correct. Notice how our definition broadens to include more cases of what we would consider justice. But we might still criticize this new definition by asking, for example, what if my friend—a highly respected gentleman, thoroughly responsible citizen—wishes to build his house in such a location that it would almost assuredly cause flooding to the houses of other highly responsible citizens when heavy rains hit.

SANTAYANA: Maybe our definition should be something akin to "justice is the largest number of responsible citizens getting what they deserve given the practical limitations of any situation."

JAMES: Okay. Note that with each iteration we are generating a broader, more inclusive concept of justice. In theory, then, shouldn't a dialectical process ultimately lead us to the broadest possible, all-inclusive concept from which all more limited concepts and ideas originate?

SANTAYANA: And if there's a grand unifying concept at the heart of the universe, mustn't there also be a grand mind or consciousness capable of understanding that concept?

JAMES: Well . . . yes . . . that was the conclusion that Bishop Berkeley arrived at, only using a somewhat different line of reasoning.

SANTAYANA: Oh . . . ?

JAMES: Berkeley argued that for something to exist it must be perceived. In fact, I would agree with him on that point, only rather than using the narrow term "perceived," I would say "experienced."

SANTAYANA: Right, of course . . .

JAMES: However, this raises the dilemma of the self—the one doing the perceiving or experiencing.

SANTAYANA: Why is the perceiver a dilemma?

JAMES: Well . . . if something must be perceived for it to exist, doesn't that mean that for me to exist as a perceiver, some larger consciousness must be perceiving me? I must be an idea in someone's mind for me to exist, just as that tree over there must be an idea in my head, or someone's head, for it to exist.

SANTAYANA: Ahhh . . . and so for Berkeley, being the good Anglican Bishop that he was, the answer to this was the mind of God.

JAMES: Right. God was the Absolute Mind . . . the ever-constant perceiver who ensured that the universe, and all of us *in* the universe, remained in existence. So whether you come at it from the rationalist, dialectical point of view or the perceptual, idealist point of view, you end up with a great Absolute Mind as the ultimate unifying principle of the universe.

SANTAYANA: But I take it that you're skeptical of this great Absolute Mind.

JAMES: The Great Unifying Mind is a compelling notion, in *theory*, but I don't see how it has much practical use. Do we have any experience of being an idea in someone else's head? I certainly don't feel as if I'm "held into being" by some Great Mind. Do you?

SANTAYANA: No . . . I don't think so. I'm not even sure what that might feel like.

JAMES: Precisely . . . so this is one of the reasons that the Great One, or the Absolute Mind of Idealism, has never appealed to me. There are other problems as well . . .

SANTAYANA: Such as . . . ?

JAMES: The universe is filled with contradiction. A man can be both generous and stingy on the same day. The same rose that inspires life with its lovely flower harbors death with its thorns. These contradictions can be connected . . . interrelated to one another . . . but they cannot be *unified* into a single thing. No mind can hold two contradictory thoughts, A and not-A, and unify them.

SANTAYANA: So you would say that there is interrelatedness in the universe, but not monistic unity.

JAMES: Correct.

SANTAYANA: You said there were other adversaries. Idealists on the left . . . who threatens from the right?

JAMES: Materialists and Positivists. Idealists want to reduce the universe to a single thought or mind. Materialists and Positivists want to reduce the world to a single substance.

SANTAYANA: A single substance?

JAMES: Yes. Mindless matter. Ultimately, for them, everything in the universe is mindless matter, blindly following the laws of physics.

SANTAYANA: Including you and me—correct?

JAMES: That would be the logical conclusion of their reductionistic thinking.

SANTAYANA: They would seem to have the weight of science on their side.

JAMES: It would seem . . .

SANTAYANA: I detect skepticism in your tone . . .

JAMES: Perceptive, Mr. Santayana. Do you experience yourself . . . or me . . . or your pet terrier as being nothing more than mindless matter blindly following the laws of physics?

SANTAYANA: No, it certainly doesn't seem that way.

JAMES: So along with the Idealists and with equal vigor, the Materialists cry out, "Experience be damned! We are machines and must boldly face that stark reality."

SANTAYANA: And in response you reply . . . ?

JAMES: "Take experience seriously!" That's what I say . . . again and again . . . to little avail.

SANTAYANA: But if the Materialists have the heavy weight of science on their side, and the only counterclaim one can make is that their view just *feels wrong*, then can they be blamed for being unmoved?

JAMES: Yes! Yes! They most certainly can be blamed. *Feeling wrong* is not a trivial counterclaim.

SANTAYANA: It's not . . . ?

JAMES: Is consciousness trivial?

SANTAYANA: Well . . . I'm not sure . . .

JAMES: Well, let me provide you with some assurance. My claim is that consciousness is not trivial. It is significant, and when we ask what is consciousness? The answer is—a feeling! It is my feeling of *knowing*. My experience of knowing! If all I am is mindless matter, then how can I possibly have this experience of knowing? How can a conscious mind be nothing but unconscious matter?

SANTAYANA: I see . . .

JAMES: You seem very impressed by what the "heavy weight of science," says. However, Mr. Santayana, you should ponder for a moment that there would be no science without consciousness. Our feeling of knowing was responsible for creating that great *weight of science*.

SANTAYANA: I see . . . yes of course. So . . . I'm trying to put this all together in my head . . .

JAMES: (sigh) Excellent . . .

SANTAYANA: So you reject the material unification of the universe—in other words, the reduction of the entire universe to matter—because in doing so consciousness is excluded.

JAMES: Yes.

SANTAYANA: But what if we just add consciousness to the universe—as dualists do. Can we say that ultimately the universe reduces to mind and matter?

JAMES: Well, we can try . . .

SANTAYANA: Again, I detect that skepticism in your voice.

JAMES: And again, I congratulate your perceptiveness. Yes . . . yes . . . many folks through the ages have argued that the universe can't be reduced to a single thing. Like me, they reject monism, whether it be materialistic monism or some kind of spiritual or conceptual monism.

SANTAYANA: Okay . . . ?

JAMES: Usually if monism is rejected, some form of dualism is accepted. The universe isn't one thing, its two things: mind and matter, soul and stuff . . . however you want to describe it. I reject monism, but dualism is unsatisfactory as well.

SANTAYANA: Why so?

JAMES: Because I don't experience mind *or* matter. I don't even experience mind *and* matter. I experience . . . *all of us* experience minds *of* matter. Or put another way, matter *with* minds.

SANTAYANA: Minds of matter? Matter with minds? I'm not sure . . .

JAMES: We experience minds made of matter. Minds directing matter. The two are intertwined in our experience. "There goes a big piece of matter with a mind in it"—that's what you and I are experiencing day after day.

SANTAYANA: Right. I see what you're saying. Our experience is not of mind and matter as distinct separate entities but of agents—other people, animals—whose minds interact with their physical bodies. Directing those bodies to behave one way or another.

JAMES: Precisely. And if we assume these are two distinct things, then it raises the serious problem of how an immaterial mind can direct a material body. But I don't think they are two distinct things. We certainly don't experience them as such.

SANTAYANA: So if dualism isn't the answer, then what is?

JAMES: Pluralism, Mr. Santayana . . . pluralism. Why not take universe to be . . . *as* we experience it?

SANTAYANA: And we experience it as . . . ?

JAMES: . . . as a multiplicity of different things. Maybe we should take that experience seriously.

SANTAYANA: But doesn't that just bring us back to my original concern?

JAMES: You worry that pluralism means . . . fragmentation . . . disunity . . . forces forever contesting with one another and therefore no hope of . . . peaceful coexistence?

SANTAYANA: Yes. Doesn't monism . . . or even dualism . . . reassure us that there is a fundamental commonality shared by all aspects of the universe? And if we can somehow harness that commonality, we'll find a basis for greater cooperation.

JAMES: I think you misunderstand the implications of pluralism. They're nowhere near as pessimistic as you suppose.

SANTAYANA: Oh . . . ?

JAMES: Pluralism rejects uniformity, but that does not mean disconnection or disintegration.

SANTAYANA: How so?

JAMES: (sighs, thinking) Hmm . . . where to begin? Let's start where we always should start, with experience. Describe your experience as you're having it at this moment.

SANTAYANA: Well . . . I'm aware of you . . . of our discussion . . . of my thoughts as I struggle to make sense of our discussion . . . of . . . the breeze . . . the birds singing and fluttering about . . . the smell of something burning . . . do you smell that . . . ?

JAMES: Yes, I noticed that as well. Let's hope it's under control. I'm comforted by the fact that it seems to be in the direction of campus rather than my house.

SANTAYANA: Right.

JAMES: So it is obvious that at any moment in time, experience has many aspects . . . it is an ongoing flux of different signals, some of which I attend to and others I ignore . . . at this moment your voice, in the next, my thoughts, then the burning smell and so forth.

SANTAYANA: Yes, that is the feel of it.

JAMES: But in another sense, experience is one thing . . . it is *experience.*

SANTAYANA: Well . . . yes, I suppose.

JAMES: If you close your eyes and merely let experience happen, without focusing on any one thing, without labeling anything as "voice," or "thought," or "burning smell,"—even if that state last only a moment, you would still, in that moment, be having an experience—wouldn't you agree?

SANTAYANA: Yes . . . I suppose so.

JAMES: This might be called a "pure experience"—the experience you have prior to any conceptual analysis of it.

SANTAYANA: Okay . . . ?

JAMES: I contend that this . . . pure experience . . . this is the most fundamental aspect of the universe . . . not mind, not matter . . . but pure experience. So a critic latching on to this fact might very well accuse me of being the worst kind of hypocrite—he who excoriates the monism of his enemies only to produce one of his own . . . a monism of pure experience.

SANTAYANA: Well . . . yes, if the universe reduces to a single thing that you call pure experience, then that would seem to be a form of monism.

JAMES: But out of pure experience plentitude arises—birds sing, thoughts meander, objects burn, and on and on. So what pure experience reveals itself to be is a multifaceted *potential* from which an almost unlimited array of *actual* experiences can emerge.

SANTAYANA: A mysterious thing, this pure experience.

JAMES: Mysterious, but undeniably real because it is the source of everything we call *real*.

SANTAYANA: So the universe is a single thing, but this single thing is multifaceted.

JAMES: Yes . . . and every time we grasp pure experience, and we analyze it into this or that . . . a bird, a voice, a thought . . . a burning thing . . . we necessarily miss something else that it is or that it could be. No single interpretation, conceptualization, or perspective on pure experience . . . and therefore on the universe . . . can capture its totality. Something is always missing. It's always . . . never, not quite.

SANTAYANA: Never . . . not quite . . . I'm not sure what you mean?

JAMES: Hmm . . . think about this, for example . . . Plato thought that the world ultimately reduced to mathematics. God is mathematician in the Platonic view. But if you look at the world exclusively in mathematical terms, is something not lost?

SANTAYANA: I suppose . . .

JAMES: How about a symphony . . . ? Mozart's requiem . . .

SANTAYANA: Mozart's requiem . . . what . . . ?

JAMES: I could take Mozart's requiem and translate it entirely into mathematical terms . . . the time signatures, the rhythm changes, the frequency ratios of the chords, their duration and decay functions . . . I'm sure we could work out an entire mathematical expression that captures the elaborate physics of that symphony.

SANTAYANA: Okay . . . and suppose we had such a mathematical expression . . . you contend that something would be missing from it?

JAMES: Yes. The music! The experience of the symphony itself. The math tells me nothing of how the music affects me . . . my emotions . . . my body. I weep because of the music in my ear, not the math on the page.

SANTAYANA: By the same token, then, if we think about the symphony exclusively in terms of the music, then we'll be missing something as well . . . no?

JAMES: Intriguing point. Yes, I believe so. Think about the experience a naïve listener has compared to someone who has studied Mozart's life and personality. For the naïve listener, the music may be beautiful, but the subtleties of it that convey the agony and struggle he went through in composing it may be missed.

SANTAYANA: And you believe that what applies to a Mozart symphony generalizes to our entire experience of the world.

JAMES: There are myriad ways that we can understand the world. A vast array of systems, perspectives, and approaches we can use for explaining and understanding it. An economist looks at the world as a complex of set of market forces . . . supply and demand . . . consumer trends . . . trade balances and imbalances and so forth. But from a lens this broad, one cannot see the brain chemistry animating each consumer or business owner.

SANTAYANA: And if we focus our lens on brain chemistry . . .

JAMES: We'll miss the context surrounding that brain. How the strict Calvinist upbringing of one child shaped an entirely different set of chemical processes in his brain compared to the permissive Unitarian atmosphere of the neighbor's child.

SANTAYANA: If we side with Freud and believe that unconscious motives drive behavior then . . .

JAMES: We'll miss how immediate rewards and punishments were responsible for the action right before our eyes. If we focus entirely on history, then we miss the *now*. If we see nothing but the *now*, we miss how the future is unfolding in front of us. If all is random, we miss the pattern. If all is preplanned, we miss the serendipitous. No single system, perspective, or approach can apprehend the totality of experience. The universe presents itself to us as a plurality because it is. But this is more than the human mind can comprehend, so we reduce . . . we simplify . . . so that we can understand and function . . . moment by moment, but always . . . in each moment, we're missing something.

SANTAYANA: Is there any way to recapture what is lost?

JAMES: To some extent . . . yes. We can broaden our perspective. We can see more and more . . . but in the end, I don't think any one person can ever comprehend the totality of experience.

SANTAYANA: So how do we see more?

JAMES: By understanding the connections among the universe's plenitudes.

SANTAYANA: Connections? What do you mean?

JAMES: Well . . . let's revisit Mozart for a moment.

SANTAYANA: Okay . . . we had concluded, I think, that understanding his requiem from a purely mathematical perspective would leave us with no understanding of the musical experience.

JAMES: Right. But saying that we miss the music if we reduce the symphony to math does not mean that there is no relation between the math and the music.

SANTAYANA: So the math and music are different, but they might be related.

JAMES: Yes. The math shows us how the relationships of different sound frequencies create more consonant or more dissonate chords, and those chords in turn generate tension or relaxation in our bodies leading to different emotional responses as we listen.

SANTAYANA: Yes . . . I'm sure the rhythm changes also have some mathematical basis and seeing that laid out in numbers or in a formula gives us greater insight into how the timing changes affect emotional responses.

JAMES: Correct. Earlier I said that looking at the world through the lens of economics may miss the role of brain chemistry. But that doesn't mean that brain chemistry does not intersect with economics. A new consumer trend might arise because a product stimulates our brain in a positive way.

SANTAYANA: So the universe is pluralistic . . . but interconnected.

JAMES: Yes . . . it is as we experience it. We experience the universe as a complex array of many different objects, systems, energies, possibilities, explanatory principles—none of which entirely captures the totality of the universe or of our experience of the universe, but all of which share a vast network of interconnections.

SANTAYANA: And it is in these interconnections that you would claim some form of unity can emerge.

JAMES: Unity . . . ? Maybe *integration* is a better way to think of it.

SANTAYANA: It seems to me that as one becomes more educated and grows more aware of the multiple perspectives from which we can understand the universe . . . this gives one a greater capacity for grasping those interconnections.

JAMES: Yes, knowing the math behind Mozart's music can give one a greater appreciation for the experience of hearing the music. Math can't replace it, but it could enhance it.

SANTAYANA: But even among the most worldly of us, is there not always a bias in how we understand the world?

JAMES: Yes. I think it is a common human weakness that afflicts everyone regardless of background . . . a blindness of sorts. We naturally assume that others see the world as we do. I confess to falling prey to this on many occasions.

SANTAYANA: Oh . . . what do you mean?

JAMES: I recall a trip I took once to the mountains of North Carolina . . .

SANTAYANA: . . . . A hiking trip, I presume. I have heard that you're an avid outdoorsman.

JAMES: Yes, I find spending time in nature is refreshing . . . exhilarating. It never fails to heighten my senses and raise my spirits. But on this particular excursion what I saw was distressing.

SANTAYANA: Oh . . . ?

JAMES: Large swaths of the forest were cut and laid bare. To my eyes, it was a scarred and pitiful land. I could not fathom why anyone would engage in such destruction, nor how anyone could stand to live in its proximity. To bear that broken-hearted sight each morning would wreck my soul.

SANTAYANA: Sure, I can understand your reaction.

JAMES: But when I questioned the locals about it, their view was very different . . . quite unexpected.

SANTAYANA: Really? How so?

JAMES: For the humble settlers there . . . what they saw was the toil and sweat they had expended to build their homesteads. It was their duty to their children and grandchildren to make the land safe and livable. They viewed it with pride.

SANTAYANA: I see . . . interesting how the same experience can be understood so differently.

JAMES: Yes. To get the widest . . . the deepest view of the world, we have no choice but to rely on others. We must do what we can to broaden our perspective, but we will never experience the world in exactly the same way as others. We need others' experience to augment our own.

SANTAYANA: I imagine people of different professional backgrounds can have widely different experiences of the world.

JAMES: Sure, the lawyer, the laborer, the scientists, the artist . . . they all experience the world differently. In fact, it would be more accurate to say that they all experience their certain slice of the world. The artist and scientist both look upon the pond teeming with life and energy but experience two very different versions of it.

SANTAYANA: So before the scientist pronounces what he believes to be the truth about the pond, he might do well to consult with the artist and vice-versa.

JAMES: Yes. And then in mutual cooperation, the two should look for the interconnections between their two *truths* of the pond.

SANTAYANA: It seems that your belief in a pluralistic universe naturally makes the case for democratic forms of governance over tyranny or monarchy.

JAMES: Oh yes . . . the fairest, most effective laws and policies are more likely to emerge when many viewpoints are taken into consideration. A king, even if he is a philosopher king, still only sees his slice of the universe.

SANTAYANA: So a wise king might be better than a tyrant, but a representative council would be better than either.

JAMES: If that council brings varied experiences into their deliberations, then yes, I'd prefer that. I believe one of the great lessons of pluralism is the essentiality of community in human life.

SANTAYANA: But how can we achieve a well-functioning community when everyone's experience is so varied? How can they relate to one another?

JAMES: Culture.

SANTAYANA: Culture? What do you mean?

JAMES: To create community, humans have constructed an agreed-upon set of norms or beliefs to shape their understanding of the world. Any community, tribe, or nation will have its own culture, its way of interpreting experience.

SANTAYANA: So you're saying that culture is, in a sense, a form of wisdom—a consensus view on how individuals in a community should interpret their experiences so that they can communicate, cooperate, and empathize with one another.

JAMES: Sure. I think the same process occurs at various scales—within families, among professional colleagues, at a factory, or in a business. They all must establish some common worldview so that the varied experiences of the individuals involved don't become so divergent that the group no longer functions effectively.

SANTAYANA: So an important part of community formation is to place limits on experience . . . to, in a way, pare down the pluralism.

JAMES: I wouldn't call it placing limits on experience, instead it's more about placing limits on how people understand their experience . . . the labels and concepts they use to interpret it. This isn't necessarily a bad thing . . .

SANTAYANA: But it could become extreme—no? Rigid dogmas could emerge, and reasonable dissent could be quashed.

JAMES: I agree. Those are problems. Cultures can become ossified. They can become so concerned with upholding order that they fail to adapt to change.

SANTAYANA: And thus, the common worldview that culturally connects people no longer functions as a network of cooperative relationships but instead becomes a noose that enforces a mindless conformity.

JAMES: That is a danger.

SANTAYANA: So how can this be avoided?

JAMES: There must always be a value placed on the experience of the individual, even when that experience is divergent from group norms. If we look at history, I believe there's evidence that it has been the divergent views of individuals that are responsible for shifting a culture in innovative and adaptive ways.

SANTAYANA: Someone such as Darwin in our own time, or Copernicus or Dante in centuries past.

JAMES: Yes. You might think of the cultural worldview as the established norm or mean value for how experience should be understood. Individual divergence keeps the mean value from becoming frozen . . . it keeps it shifting around somewhat so that it can adapt to changing circumstances.

SANTAYANA: So a healthy balance must be struck. Too much variability in worldviews causes dissolution, but too little causes ossification.

JAMES: Yes . . . the right balance is necessary for a healthy community.

SANTAYANA: Professor James . . . I'm still not entirely sure what to make of pluralism. To accept that the universe simply is . . . many . . . and not ultimately some single, unified thing . . .

JAMES: Ask yourself this: Is the notion that the universe is a plurality, as our experience indicates . . . is that any less plausible as a working hypothesis that the notions of monism or dualism?

SANTAYANA: I suppose not.

JAMES: And I hope I have shown that the acceptance of pluralism has some practical ramifications that might make it more useful than monism or dualism, once we recognize that the universe is an *interconnected* plurality.

SANTAYANA: I shall ponder upon those interconnections. Ahh . . . I see your house just up ahead. You have a beautiful home, Professor James. It must be a joy to return to it each evening.

JAMES: Yes. Thank you (then with modest laughter). You see a beautiful home, Mr. Santayana. I see a year's worth of planning and labor that mysteriously resulted in two mismatched front windows.

SANTAYANA: More evidence of pluralism.

JAMES: Indeed.

Chapter 5

To Be Free[1]

Topic: Freedom of the will

Student: W. E. B. Du Bois

Outline:

Does self-destructive obstinance prove free will?
The meaning of determinism
   Is novelty real?
   Does the past predict the future?
   Chance and irrationality
The role of consciousness in the universe
   Regret in a deterministic world
   Value in a deterministic world
The causal power of freedom
Attention and freedom
Freedom and self-improvement
Believing and practicing freedom

W. E. B. Du Bois

W. E. B. Du Bois was born on February 23, 1863, in Great Barrington, Massachusetts. He graduated from the historically black university of Fisk University in Nashville, Tennessee, in 1888 and went on to complete a PhD at Harvard in 1895, where he took classes with William James. He became an important leader in the civil rights movement in the early twentieth century and shared in the creation of the National Association for the Advancement of Colored People (NAACP) in 1909. He was a highly respected sociologist, historian, editor, and author whose

---

[1] Taken largely from James's essay "The dilemma of determinism," from *The will to believe and other essays in popular philosophy* (New York: Longmans, Green, and Co., 1896), and chapter 11 (Attention) from *Principles of psychology*.

book *The Souls of Black Folk* (1903) is considered a milestone in African American literature.

William James scans the leafy Harvard quad as he exists the lecture hall. He perches his hat firmly upon his head and begins to walk home after a long day of teaching. As he rounds the corner onto Oxford Street, a lone student approaches him. James recognizes him immediately—W. E. B. Du Bois, one of the few black students that James has taught.

DU BOIS: Ahh . . . Professor James.

JAMES: (tipping his hat slightly) Mr. Du Bois. How are you this fine afternoon?

DU BOIS: Very well. And you?

JAMES: Invigorated by the breeze. After spending the day in dank, stuffy lecture halls, it feels good to be outdoors.

DU BOIS: How opportune that our paths have crossed. There's something I've been wanting to discuss with you.

JAMES: Is that right?

DU BOIS: Yes . . . an issue you raised a few lectures ago that has been on my mind for some time now . . .

JAMES: Oh . . . ?

DU BOIS: Yes . . . yes . . . something I've been turning over in my head, and I think I may have arrived at a solution. But I'd like to get your opinion on it.

JAMES: I'm paid for my opinions.

DU BOIS: Oh . . . one thing first . . . if it's not too much trouble . . .

JAMES: What?

DU BOIS: You're heading to your house on Irving Street, I presume.

JAMES: That was my plan . . .

DU BOIS: But . . . well . . . umm . . . you can get to Irving from either Oxford or Divinity, I believe.

JAMES: Yes, that's true.

DU BOIS: Would you mind so much if we backtracked a bit and got onto Divinity rather than staying on Oxford?

JAMES: No . . . either suits my purposes.

DU BOIS: I'm grateful. I have another appointment and Divinity gets me there more easily than Oxford.

JAMES: Glad to be of service. Now . . . that issue on which you believe you have a solution . . .

DU BOIS: Well . . . it's the matter of freedom . . . of free will that you were speaking of . . .

James stops in his tracks and jabs Du Bois with a skeptical glare.

JAMES: Mr. Du Bois, you can't be serious.

DU BOIS: (becoming a bit sheepish) Well . . . yes . . . I think I may have . . .

JAMES: . . . a solution. A solution to the problem of free will. You've figured it out.

DU BOIS: Well . . . yes . . . have you ever considered . . .

JAMES: Mr. Du Bois . . . you believe you've come up with a way of proving . . . or disproving that we have free will?

DU BOIS: Well . . . yes . . . *proving*, I'd say. Have you thought about . . . ?

JAMES: You think you can prove the existence of free will?

DU BOIS: (becoming a bit annoyed) Well . . . if you'd give me a chance . . .

JAMES: It's an impossible . . . (slight laughter) . . . okay, Mr. Du Bois, let me hear it. What insight have you come to that has eluded all great minds up to now?

DU BOIS: Actually . . . (reaching into the breast pocket of his coat) I developed the germ of the idea from this article I ran across. You see, there was this Mr. Mathias . . . William Mathias . . .

Du Bois unfolds a paper and begins reading.

DU BOIS: "Longtime North Warwickshire resident William Mathias died today at the age of ninety-two. Mathias, a teacher and part-time dairyman, was best known for his longstanding fight with the local shire council over the use of a footpath crossing his land. Though the footpath was designated a public right-of-way, Mathias grew frustrated with the amount of traffic crossing his pasture and disturbing his herd. In defiance of the council orders, he built a wall blocking access to the footpath, preventing his neighbors and other travelers from reaching the nearby village. Each time the wall was demolished, Mathias would rebuild it."

JAMES: Stubborn chap . . . but how does this . . . ?

DU BOIS: . . . Uh . . . well . . . you'll see, let me go on . . .

James sighs in assent.

DU BOIS: "Though Mathias was jailed and fined repeatedly for his obstinance, he never gave up the fight. In the end, it led him to bankruptcy and the loss of his home and farm."

JAMES: (puzzled) Well . . . that's a fascinating little anecdote about dear old Mr. Mathias, but its relevance to free will evades me. Enlighten if you will, Mr. Du Bois.

DU BOIS: Mr. Mathias appears to be exemplary of what I would call self-destructive stubbornness.

JAMES: Indeed.

DU BOIS: Would you agree with me that this trait, while present in humans, is unlikely to be found in any other creature?

JAMES: Agreed. Most other animals are smart enough not to doom themselves through their own efforts.

DU BOIS: Yet here is Mr. Mathias doing exactly that. Violating nature's most fundamental law . . .

JAMES: Nature's most fundamental law?

DU BOIS: Yes . . . survival! Stay alive.

JAMES: But there's nothing in the story claiming his row with the council specifically led to his death. In fact, didn't you say he was ninety . . . something . . .

DU BOIS: Ninety-two.

JAMES: Right . . . ninety-two when he died. That's a ripe old age.

DU BOIS: True. But his actions were clearly self-destructive. Defending his stretch of the pathway cost him his entire estate.

JAMES: Yes . . . and I'm sure we could dig up other examples where someone's obstinance was indeed fatal. So your point, if I'm reading you correctly, is that in a deterministic world—a world without freedom—no one should be able to behave contrary to their own survival interests. Is that the idea?

DU BOIS: Certainly. It seems to me that the most fundamental of all natural laws would be that of self-preservation. If the world were strictly deterministic, then we ought not be able to violate that law. Yet examples of self-destructive obstinance obviously show the fallacy of this reasoning.

JAMES: The fallacy of that reasoning . . . not necessarily the fallacy of determinism.

DU BOIS: What . . . ? I'm not sure I follow . . .

JAMES: I think you misunderstand the basic premise of deterministic thinking.

DU BOIS: Oh . . . ?

JAMES: The question isn't whether Mr. Mathias is or is not free to act contrary to his self-interests. The question is whether Mr. Mathias, given his biological and psychological makeup, could have acted any differently than he did.

DU BOIS: But of course he could have. He could have realized his own foolishness.

JAMES: But how do we know that? Mr. Mathias acted as he did. That is simply a matter of fact. That his actions, in your judgment, go contrary to some supposed law of nature, is of little consequence. The determinist would merely claim that Mr. Mathias *had no choice* but to act contrary to his self-interest. Some of us are just bound to be fools!

DU BOIS: (puzzled) But . . . couldn't that argument be . . . turned against itself?

JAMES: What do you mean?

DU BOIS: Well . . . you say we can't be sure he freely chose to be a fool. He might have been determined to be such.

JAMES: Yes . . . ?

DU BOIS: Couldn't I just as readily assert that we can't be sure that he was *determined* to be a fool? He might very well have freely chosen such a course.

JAMES: Yes. Precisely. Now you understand my initial skepticism when you claimed to have proven the existence of free will. Philosophers have been debating this issue for centuries. It's highly unlikely that you and I, and our dear departed Mr. Mathias, are going to settle it on our walk to Irving Street.

DU BOIS: I see. So if it's an intractable dilemma . . . this issue of free will . . . then is there any point in even discussing it?

JAMES: Forgive the irony but . . . I think we have *no choice* but to discuss it.

DU BOIS: Really . . . and why is that?

JAMES: Because regardless of anyone's opinion on the matter, one thing is undisputable regarding free will.

DU BOIS: And what is that?

JAMES: We experience it. It is an undeniable aspect of our experience. Experience tells us that we are free. We make real choices.

DU BOIS: So why doesn't that settle the matter?

JAMES: (a modest chuckle) Honestly, I think it ought to. But over the centuries, few philosophers have found experience alone to be satisfactory as a rational defense. And so, we argue.

DU BOIS: If we can't demonstrate with certainty either the reality or nonreality of free will, then what is the basis for any argument on the issue?

JAMES: Rationality, I suppose.

DU BOIS: Rationality?

JAMES: Yes. What does reason tell us? Does the world appear to be a more reasonable place if we accept or reject freedom?

DU BOIS: And as a believer in free will, you must think the world is more reasonable with it than without it.

JAMES: Yes.

DU BOIS: How so?

JAMES: Well . . . first we must understand what determinism means. Many different forms and nuanced versions of determinism have been bandied about lately, thus making it rather confusing. But I think once you clear away the confusion there's a fundamental core to all deterministic thinking.

DU BOIS: And what is that?

JAMES: The rejection of novelty.

DU BOIS: Rejection of novelty?

JAMES: Yes. The key difference between the determinist and indeterminist is this: The determinist says that the state of the universe at any given moment dictates what can occur at any moment hence.

DU BOIS: So the past determines the future.

JAMES: Correct. The future holds no novelty, no surprises, no hidden ambiguities that could not be predicted by past conditions.

Du Bois suddenly sneezes.

DU BOIS: That was a surprise.

JAMES: Not really.

DU BOIS: Now hold on. Who could have predicted that I would have sneezed at that very moment? My health has been impeccable. I have no allergies to speak of. It's not the season for dust or spores or excessive pollen blowing about. I contend that my sneeze was a true novelty, utterly unpredictable based on past conditions.

JAMES: The determinist would disagree.

DU BOIS: On what grounds?

JAMES: The past determines the future, but our knowledge of the past is never complete. There may always be important causal factors or conditions that evade our understanding. Merely because something was unpredictable from our subjective standpoint does not mean that it was unpredictable *in principle*.

DU BOIS: So in other words, if we had complete knowledge of all the relevant factors that affect any particular outcome, we should have perfect prediction.

JAMES: Correct. The determinist argument is a theoretical argument. It does not claim that we presently know the future with certainty. It says that we could potentially know . . . someday . . . if or when our science progresses to the point of complete understanding.

DU BOIS: But the fundamental distinction, in theory at least, remains intact between the determinist and indeterminist—correct? That being that the determinist rejects the notion of any true novelty in the universe, while the indeterminist claims that novelty is not just an artifact of our ignorance but an integral reality of the universe.

JAMES: Yes. For the indeterminist, novelty is a reality. The indeterminist sees the universe as inherently possessing possibilities that exceed actualities. Something *may be*, but it did not *have to be*.

DU BOIS: Thus, we have two distinctly different visions of the universe. A deterministic vision where novelty is an illusion and an indeterministic one where novelty is real.

JAMES: Yes, and I would argue that both visions ultimately rest on the sentiments . . . the passionate natures, you might say, of the beholders.

DU BOIS: Passionate natures?

JAMES: Because neither science nor logic can convincingly settle the issue, we fall back on our gut feelings. What kind of universe do we desire? That becomes the critical question. The determinist is deeply unsettled by the prospect of a free-wheeling, chaotic, irrational universe. The indeterminist is no less upset by the prospect of a universe marching along in lockstep, so contrary to what everyday experience appears to convey.

DU BOIS: And your gut aligns with freedom . . . I take it.

JAMES: Yes, for many reasons . . . but chief among them is my belief that the determinist misunderstands what lies behind the universe's novelty.

DU BOIS: Lies behind the universe's novelty . . . ? I'm not sure I follow.

JAMES: From where do you think novelty emerges?

DU BOIS: From where . . . ? You mean what produces novelty in the universe?

JAMES: Yes.

DU BOIS: What produces novelty . . . ? Well . . . I suppose novelty arises from the many different possibilities that exist, only one of which can be actualized into a reality.

JAMES: Fine . . . fine . . . but what is it that . . . *selects*, you might say, among those different possibilities?

DU BOIS: What *selects* among the different possibilities . . . ?

JAMES: Yes . . . yes. In the indeterminist world, there are many different possibilities, poised and ready to become reality, but only one of them gets the crown. Now . . . the determinist might not find this description all that objectionable. "Sure," he might agree, "There are all these possibilities at the ready. But the choice among them has already been set by past conditions. The choice is fixed." But the indeterminist says, "No, the choice is not fixed . . . "

DU BOIS: So if the choice is not fixed, then for the indeterminist there must be . . . varying probabilities at play . . . even a certain element of chance . . .

JAMES: (with satisfaction) Exactly. A certain element of *chance* must come into play. That's what the indeterminist sees that is wholly unacceptable to the determinist—chance!

DU BOIS: And so the determinist is uncomfortable with freedom because it introduces chance into the universe.

JAMES: Yes. I think an indeterministic sees chance as an irrational, chaotic force—and if we admit that chance is an integral part of the universe, then it makes the universe fundamentally irrational. Science can never explain the totality of the universe when chance is an inalienable part of it.

DU BOIS: I see. And if in his gut the determinist wants the universe to be fully amenable to the scientific method . . .

JAMES: Then he finds chance a bitter enemy that must be opposed at every turn.

DU BOIS: I see.

JAMES: But this antipathy is misplaced. It's based on a misunderstanding of what chance means.

DU BOIS: A misunderstanding . . . ?

JAMES: Yes. The determinist is convinced that chance is a positive or additive feature of the universe.

DU BOIS: Positive . . . additive? What do you mean?

JAMES: A feature that introduces or adds some characteristic to universe. This is not the case. Chance is not a positive feature of the universe, it's a neutral feature. It adds nothing. It merely compromises predictive power.

DU BOIS: I don't follow . . .

JAMES: Saying that something occurred "by chance" does not inherently make the resulting outcome irrational. It only makes it unpredictable. No chaos or irrationality need be assumed when chance selects an outcome any more than when rational deliberation selects the outcome.

DU BOIS: But that seems to be an assumption on your part. How can we be sure chance is not introducing irrationality . . .

JAMES: Well . . . let's think about it for a moment . . . what if . . . ? Wait . . . earlier, when we first encountered one another on Oxford Street . . . we had to decide whether to remain on Oxford or to take Divinity—recall?

DU BOIS: Yes . . . you were kind enough to agree to take Divinity because of an appointment I have later.

JAMES: Right . . . so we selected Divinity for a perfectly valid reason—to accommodate your appointment. The selection was not by chance but by reason . . . you would agree?

DU BOIS: Yes, I agree. Our presence here on Divinity is not a matter of chance, not at all.

JAMES: But let's suppose otherwise.

DU BOIS: Suppose otherwise?

JAMES: Yes. Let's suppose that you had no appointment and that our encounter had occurred at the intersection of Oxford and Divinity. Envision us standing there . . . Oxford extending out one direction and Divinity the other.

DU BOIS: Okay . . . ?

JAMES: We stand utterly perplexed by the choice we must make—Oxford or Divinity . . . ? How to decide? Finally, one of us in frustration pulls out a coin, flips it into the air, and announces, "heads, Oxford; tails, Divinity."

DU BOIS: (modest laughter) . . . Alright . . . I see, and how does that monumental coin toss turn out?

JAMES: Well . . . Divinity, of course. We end up with the same outcome as before, only this time for no reason other than chance.

DU BOIS: I'm struggling to get the point.

JAMES: We have examples of two different universes. One where Divinity was a rational choice, the other where it was a chance occurrence. Which one is the rational universe, and which one is the irrational one?

DU BOIS: They're both the same.

JAMES: Exactly. Anyone observing the result after the fact could not tell the difference. The two universes are identical. Chance introduced no inherent irrationality into the universe where it was allowed to function.

DU BOIS: I can see where that might soothe somewhat the determinist's fears of an irrational universe. But the unpredictability associated with chance still places limits on science—does it not? If the determinist's goal is for science to unfailingly explain the universe, then chance still stands as an obstacle.

JAMES: The determinist's dream of a perfect science may not be attainable. But perfection is probably not a realistic goal for science. Science need not be perfect to be highly useful.

DU BOIS: I see . . .

JAMES: But the limits placed on science by chance are small compared to those imposed by another factor present in our universe.

DU BOIS: What's that?

JAMES: Consciousness.

DU BOIS: Consciousness? How does consciousness place limits on science?

JAMES: Consciousness introduces choices into the universe that are made based on subjective wants, goals, and desires. These aren't selections that are necessarily irrational or chance based, but they are subjective. I don't see how the objective methods of science can penetrate the subjective world of conscious decisions.

DU BOIS: So in your view, a universe where conscious choices are made will always be a universe where science falls short of a complete predictive power.

JAMES: Yes . . . so the determinist's goal of a complete science is, ironically, irrational.

DU BOIS: Interesting that you mention consciousness, because this brings me to another concern I have always had about determinism.

JAMES: And what is that?

DU BOISE: It seems to me that if the universe were truly a deterministic one, then we would have to attribute our experience of free will . . . the feeling that I'm actually making my own choices . . . we'd have to dismiss that as a grand illusion. Nature has played a great hoax on us.

JAMES: Agreed. A hoax about one of the most . . . maybe *the* most . . . basic attribute of humanity—our sense of agency. It's hard for me to imagine that we could be such a well-adapted species with so deep a flaw built into our experience.

DU BOIS: So our general assumption should be that experience can be trusted.

JAMES: Until convincingly proved otherwise, yes. I believe so. And it's not just our feeling of being free that is relevant to the issue of determinism versus indeterminism, there's another aspect of our experience that becomes very hard to explain if the universe was truly deterministic.

DU BOIS: What is that?

JAMES: Our emotional lives.

DU BOIS: Emotional lives? What do you mean?

JAMES: Our emotions seem ill-suited for a deterministic world. Especially our feelings of regret.

DU BOIS: Regret?

JAMES: A curious emotion, don't you think?

DU BOIS: Curious . . . ? I can't say that I have ever considered it as so. Instead it seems to me to be a very useful emotion. We commit some lamentable act . . . some trespass of moral or social norms, and our guts tell us that we have sinned . . . we have fallen short of the standards that we and others hold for us.

JAMES: Indeed . . . I agree, a very functional emotion. Our regret often compels us to seek forgiveness or to make amends or restitution, and in doing so we repair social bonds . . . we restore our good standing with colleagues and friends.

DU BOIS: The lessons learned from a regrettable episode could also spur self-improvement. We put ourselves on guard not to make the same error a second time.

JAMES: So we agree that regret, while unpleasant when we endure it, nonetheless serves us well as moral and social beings.

DU BOIS: Fully agree . . . so again, your characterization as curious seems odd.

JAMES: I call it curious, not because I fail to see its utility, but because when we consider regret in the context of a deterministic world, it seems to have no place.

DU BOIS: No place . . . ?

JAMES: Consider for a moment that regret does not merely apply to situations of our own making. We regret many things . . . not infrequently events over which we have no control.

DU BOIS: Such as . . . ?

JAMES: Suppose a dear friend was to accompany me on a hiking trip that the two of us had planned for some time.

DU BOIS: Okay . . . ?

JAMES: On the morning the trip was to commence, my friend contacts me and says that he must cancel the trip because his child has had a bad accident and is in the hospital teetering between life and death.

DU BOIS: I see.

JAMES: I'm likely to tell my friend how saddened I am over this most *regrettable* turn of events.

DU BOIS: Yes, I would agree that is a regrettable occurrence.

JAMES: Regrettable, but not an event that was in any way brought about by a moral infraction on my part.

DU BOIS: So your point is that we feel regret not just for our own shortcomings but for events that are merely matters of fate.

JAMES: Yes . . . curious, I think.

DU BOIS: Curious because we feel regret in situations where we can offer no restitution.

JAMES: True . . . but I think curious for an even more fundamental reason.

DU BOIS: That being . . . ?

JAMES: If determinism is true, then my friend's misfortune was simply *meant to be* from the dawn of time. It could not have turned out any other way.

DU BOIS: And you think regret is somehow misplaced when applied to situations that could not have been different.

JAMES: Yes. Regret only makes sense if a different outcome was a real possibility. I regret my friend's misfortune because I'm convinced that a world where his child suffered no accident and we enjoyed a refreshing hike in the New Hampshire mountains was a viable, possible reality, not an illusion.

DU BOIS: And because that reality was thwarted, and in its place a far more unpleasant one was realized, there's truly something to regret.

JAMES: Exactly. Our experience of regret is a supreme waste of emotional energy in a world where everything that happens could not have been any other way.

DU BOIS: But must it be the case that the entirety of our emotional life is a perfect fit with reality? Maybe regret is sometimes a . . . misguided emotion.

JAMES: Misguided . . . ?

DU BOIS: Maybe it's based on how we perceive the world to be, not on how it really is.

JAMES: I suppose that's possible. But the dilemma goes far deeper than just the feeling of regret. Regret is just . . . the tip of the iceberg, you might say.

DU BOIS: You think regret is just the symptom of a much deeper problem?

JAMES: Yes . . . yes. Think for a moment of why we experience regret. What is the emotion telling us about a certain outcome?

DU BOIS: Well . . . that the outcome was . . . tragic . . . or at least far less desirable compared to another.

JAMES: Yes . . . yes! Compared to another—that's the critical point, isn't it?

DU BOIS: Well . . . yes, of course. We regret the actual outcome because we would have preferred a different one. You would have preferred that your friend's child remained healthy and happy, and that you and your friend enjoyed the long-anticipated hiking trip.

JAMES: Correct. For regret to work, you might say, as an emotion . . . for it to make any sense at all, we must have some sort of value system that triggers the emotion. A healthy child and a refreshing hiking trip are *better* outcomes than a hospitalized child and a thwarted trip. But *why* are they better? Who says they are better?

DU BOIS: Well . . . they're better because they involve pleasure and not pain . . . I suppose.

JAMES: Fine . . . fine . . . so we value pleasure over pain. But upon what basis are we doing any *valuing* at all? In a world where everything *is* exactly as it was *meant to be*, any judgments of one thing being better than another have no rational basis. Nothing could have been other than what it was.

DU BOIS: . . . And if nothing could have been other than what it was, then there's no valid comparison to be made between one outcome or another.

JAMES: Precisely. Value judgments are irrelevant in a deterministic world. Regret assumes values, and values are meaningless when things could not have been different from what they were. Yet values are central to our experience of the world.

DU BOIS: Now I'm seeing more clearly why you claimed that regret was just the tip of the iceberg. We experience regret because we have a system of values that tells us that some things . . . objects . . . events . . . outcomes and so forth are better . . . or are of greater value than others.

JAMES: Correct.

DU BOIS: And if the world is truly deterministic then explaining the origin of values becomes difficult . . .

JAMES: We would have to explain it by arguing, once again, that fundamentally human experience is based on . . . indeed, thoroughly saturated through and through by an illusion . . . the illusion that things could be different from what they are.

DU BOIS: Well . . . that could be possible—no?

JAMES: But is it more rational? We experience freedom, but we're not free. We experience values, but they don't exist. How could we be such a successful species when our experience of ourselves and our world is so utterly and deeply wrong? How can our science be so effective when our mental design is so faulty? It makes no sense to me.

DU BOIS: So you think it is simply more rational to accept that human experience is telling us something fundamentally *true* about reality.

JAMES: Yes. And there is something else about our experience of freedom that convinces me that it is more than an illusion.

DU BOIS: What is that?

JAMES: Freedom has causal power. We can use free will to transform ourselves, to make ourselves better. How can an illusion do that?

DU BOIS: What do you mean?

JAMES: Do you recall my lecture on the nature of experience?

DU BOIS: Are you referring to the . . . stream of thought . . . as you called it?

JAMES: Yes. We experience the world as an ongoing stream of sensory inputs and internal signals, and at any one moment there is far more information in the stream than can be fully processed.

DU BOIS: Yes . . . and as I recall this is where attention plays a critical role. We dice up the ongoing stream into fragments or units.

JAMES: Right. Out of the stream we isolate certain elements by paying attention to them. Do you recall how we used attention to, as you say, *dice up* the ongoing stream?

DU BOIS: You mean . . . how it is that attention goes about "deciding" what elements to isolate and what elements to ignore?

JAMES: Yes. That's the critical question. By what criterion do we allocate attention to the stream of thought?

DU BOIS: Well, if I recall correctly, it has to do with our interests . . . our desires . . . our goals.

JAMES: Yes, precisely. The mind is goal-driven. Now, there are times when attention can be reflexive. A bright flash or a loud boom will immediately draw our attention. But normally when we attend to something and sustain our attention on it, it is because whatever that object is, it serves some purpose.

DU BOIS: And when this is the case, if my memory serves, you called this an act of will.

JAMES: Yes. This is a volitional direction of attention. We chose to attend to *this* rather than *that*. Because *this* is interesting, important, it serves our goals and intentions.

DU BOIS: Are you saying that our direction of attention is a form of free will?

JAMES: I think under certain conditions, it certainly *feels* as if we are free.

DU BOIS: Under certain conditions? What conditions?

JAMES: Under conditions when our inclinations or immediate desires would have us attend to something other than what we focus on.

DU BOIS: I'm not sure I follow.

JAMES: It happens to me almost every morning this time of year.

DU BOIS: What?

JAMES: You felt the distinct chill in the air this morning, did you not?

DU BOIS: Oh, yes. I hear the first frost is headed our way soon.

JAMES: Lying comfortably in my warm bed, the prospect of arising to a freezing cold house was an unwelcome one indeed.

DU BOIS: But you arose, nonetheless.

JAMES: An act of pure will if there ever was one. I would have preferred to keep my mind focused on the comfort of my warm bed, but instead I directed my attention to my appointed responsibilities . . . to the needs of my students rather than my own desires and . . . so here we are another day at work.

DU BOIS: And so you claim that when we deliberately focus our attention on what *needs* to be done, rather than what we are *inclined* to do, we are exercising our free will.

JAMES: I would put it this way—it is when we force our attention onto that which is contrary to our immediate desires or inclinations . . . when we "gut it out" despite pain or discomfort, that is when our *experience* of freedom is most keenly felt.

DU BOIS: I see. We feel most free when we . . . *overcome obstacles*—is that what you're saying?

JAMES: Overcome obstacles—yes . . . and sometimes one's greatest obstacle is oneself. Overcoming ourselves—that's the real challenge.

DU BOIS: Overcoming ourselves? What do you mean?

JAMES: I'll use myself as an example.

DU BOIS: You used the willful direction of attention to overcome yourself . . . to make yourself better?

JAMES: Yes, most definitely.

DU BOIS: Tell me how.

JAMES: (with a sigh) . . . Tell me Mr. Du Bois, in your experience with me as a teacher, would you judge me as a man of generally optimistic or pessimistic nature?

DU BOIS: Oh . . . I would clearly say optimistic. Your lectures exude with positive energy . . . with the promise of how science and philosophy might change the world for the better and the role we students might play in that pursuit.

JAMES: Good . . . that is certainly the image I wish to project.

DU BOIS: Image . . . ? Are you implying that your optimism is more façade than character trait?

JAMES: Well . . . the difference between the two can be rather oblique.

DU BOIS: What do you mean?

JAMES: I don't believe by nature that I am truly an optimist. In my youth, I was prone to prolonged episodes of deep melancholy.

DU BOIS: Really . . . but not so much anymore?

JAMES: No, not as much.

DU BOIS: And you credit the deliberate focusing of attention as a way of curing you of your melancholy?

JAMES: Well . . . I wouldn't say *cure*, but I would say that it played a role in managing my moods and, in a general way, elevating my outlook.

DU BOIS: So what did you do?

JAMES: Even in my darkest moments, there were always certain experiences that offered me hope. The beauty of nature . . . hearing birdsong . . . the refreshing feel of a morning breeze.

DU BOIS: So you would call these things to mind when your mood started to slip?

JAMES: Yes. Call them to mind . . . force myself to pay attention to them when I was outdoors . . . force myself to get up and take a walk so I could find these things and immerse myself in them. I would tell myself, "You are free to see, to think, to experience that which is good in life and not bound to that which is dreary."

DU BOIS: Well . . . it seems to have worked.

JAMES: Saying "worked" is too conclusive. Let's say it appears to be working.

DU BOIS: Alright . . . appears to be working. By this I suppose you mean that forcing yourself to see the good in the world is something that you continually remind yourself of . . . an ongoing struggle, if you will.

JAMES: On ongoing *challenge*, I'd say. Yes, at first it requires constant reminding and effort. But humans are designed to acquire habits. It was my habit to view life pessimistically . . . to attend to that which was gloomy.

DU BOIS: And so you had to consciously break yourself of that disposition and acquire a new way of thinking about the world—is that right?

JAMES: Yes. But if you stick with it. If you force yourself to attend to the good, and you do it over and over again . . .

DU BOIS: . . . You practice it, you mean—right?

JAMES: Yes, yes, you practice it. Then over time it starts to become habit . . . a new habit . . . a healthier habit.

DU BOIS: Isn't this a bit like what an actor does? An actor takes on a new role . . . a new personality . . . and he has to see the world the way the character sees the world. He has to think like the character, react as the character would, and so forth.

JAMES: Yes and suppose that the character being portrayed is someone the actor admires . . . someone the actor wants to be more like.

DU BOIS: So in a sense you're suggesting that for purposes of self-improvement, people should pretend to be something they are not.

JAMES: "Pretend to be what they are not . . ." No. I'd rather think of it as willfully practicing to be more like the person they desire to be. Listen . . . I knew a colleague in Germany who had a terrible time with impatience. Whether it was at a restaurant or a government office or wherever, being forced to wait often caused him to go into an implacable rage. He and I were once dining with a most agreeable fellow—a Lutheran minister. And the minister told him that for years he struggled with the same problem.

DU BOIS: But the minister had overcome the problem?

JAMES: Yes. And my colleague wanted to be more like the minister. He wanted to have greater patience. So he asked the minister, "Tell me, how did you become a more patient person?"

DU BOIS: And what did the minister say?

JAMES: He said every time he was in a situation where his patience was being tried, he recited a prayer for patience. "Love is patient. Love is kind. It does not envy. It does not boast . . . ." Over and over, until he had settled his soul. And he advised my friend to try it.

DU BOIS: I see. And in reciting the prayer, he was deliberately drawing his attention away from the maddening situation and focusing instead on a more . . . shall we say, *saintly* attitude toward the world's frustrations.

JAMES: He was training himself to be more like the person he desired to be rather than the person he presently was.

DU BOIS: And with enough practice, this approach could become habit.

JAMES: Indeed, that seemed to be what happened.

DU BOIS: And what about your friend? Did this strategy work for him?

JAMES: Well, I left Germany the following day and I have not been in touch with him for quite a while. One can hope . . .

DU BOIS: These positive personal transformations that you cite—are you contending that they demonstrate the causal power of free will?

JAMES: Let's call it a hypothesis. It seems reasonable to hypothesize that the willful direction of attention can cause personal transformation. And for one to even think that he can willfully direct his attention, he must first believe that he has the freedom to do so.

DU BOIS: So free will can cause positive change, but to harness this causal power, we must believe that freedom exists.

JAMES: A bit of an irony, wouldn't you say.

DU BOIS: Yes. But then we are still left with whether there is any truth in freedom or not.

JAMES: It is either true, or it is a strangely potent and useful illusion.

DU BOIS: And you would contend that it simply makes more sense to accept it as true.

JAMES: (breaking out in laughter). Yes. But truth, Mr. Du Bois, is another matter. Well . . . (pointing to a house just ahead) my destination. And I believe you are running a tad late for an appointment.

DU BOIS: Indeed. I must bid you farewell and good evening.

JAMES: Likewise, Mr. Du Bois.

Chapter 6

Truth[1]

Morris Cohen

Morris Cohen was born in Minsk, Belarus (then part of Imperial Russia), on July 25, 1880. He moved to New York when he was twelve years old and later studied at both the City College of New York and Harvard University. At Harvard, he studied under both William James and Josiah Royce. He completed his PhD in 1906. He went on to teach philosophy at CCNY and law at the University of Chicago. Cohen was a staunch defender of academic freedom and a founding member of the American Association of University Professors, an organization dedicated to that cause. In his most influential book, *Reason and Nature* (published in 1931), Cohen argued for liberal democracy and sharply criticized both

---

[1] Taken largely from William James's *Pragmatism: A new name for some old ways of thinking* (New York: Longman Green and Co., 1907), especially chapter 6, "Pragmatism's conception of truth."

fascism and communism. Cohen was, however, equally critical of laissez-faire capitalism.

Harvard student Morris Cohen scans frantically down Oxford Street, then hastily turns and heads toward Divinity Avenue. He spots William James strolling along at a relaxed pace. He races to catch up with him.

COHEN: Professor James! Professor James!

James pauses and turns to see Cohen approaching briskly. He points a figure at the young man while examining him with a quizzical look.

JAMES: Mister . . . Cohen . . . Cohen . . . is that correct?

COHEN: Yes . . . right . . . that's me. Morris Cohen.

JAMES: Right . . . Morris Cohen. So how are you today, Mr. Cohen?

COHEN: Oh . . . fine . . . very fine . . . thank you. And yourself?

JAMES: Well, I was enjoying a solitary amble home on this fine autumn afternoon. But that has apparently come to an end. I presume there's something you wish to discuss with me.

COHEN: Ahh . . . yes. Well . . . I'm sorry if I'm disturbing you. If another time would be better . . . I could . . .

JAMES: (a modest laugh) No . . . no. Don't worry. I'm happy to entertain a little company, especially if it is motivated by a sincere quest for wisdom.

COHEN: Yes . . . yes. That is what I seek.

JAMES: Good that you found me then. I nearly took the other route home . . . down Oxford Street. Had I done that you might have missed me. Maybe fate has ordained that we should meet so that your mind might be suitably enlarged.

COHEN: I looked down Oxford for you because I've seen you walking that way before. When I didn't see you, I came this way.

JAMES: Oh, well . . . maybe fate and your dogged persistence have brought us together. In any case . . . how may I help you?

COHEN: A remark you made the other day in lecture . . . it left me quite dumfounded. I've been meaning to take it up with you, but I hadn't the occasion until now.

JAMES: Alright. So what could I have said that left you so dumfounded?

COHEN: Well . . . maybe I misheard or misunderstood you because . . . what you said . . . it seemed to make no sense.

JAMES: Trust me, Mr. Cohen, you're hardly the first to accuse me of filling young minds with nonsense. Now what exactly did I say?

COHEN: Something to the effect that . . . well . . . truth . . . that truth was like health or wealth. It's something that is *made*, not something that simply *is*.

JAMES: Spot on, Mr. Cohen. You understood me perfectly. That's what I said.

COHEN: Well . . . forgive me Professor James . . . and I mean no disrespect . . . I have great admiration for your writings, and I think you're an excellent teacher . . .

JAMES: . . . Fine, fine . . . you're forgiven . . . and I won't feel ill of you . . . now what's your objection?

COHEN: Well . . . it seems to me that statement is . . . obviously absurd. Something is either *true* or it is not true. Truth simply *is*. To say it's made is not only . . . incorrect . . . but downright dangerous.

JAMES: Dangerous? Hmm . . . why do you think that?

COHEN: If truth is something that is made, then what is there to prevent powerful people from declaring truth at their whim? If a brutal tyrant decides that he should be known as a just and compassionate ruler despite a history of violent repression, then by your definition he is free to do so . . . he's free to make truth in any form he wishes.

JAMES: Well, he's free to try. Whether he'll succeed or not is a different matter.

COHEN: But wouldn't you object and point out the falsity of his claim?

JAMES: Yes. I might.

COHEN: Then doesn't your objection prove that one cannot make truth . . . that truth is not made, it simply is.

JAMES: (a long sigh) Hmm . . . I think you're misunderstanding what I mean by *made*. I'm not saying it's made by men. I'm saying it's made by experience. We experience truth, just as we experience anything in our lives.

COHEN: Made by experience?

JAMES: Yes . . . as a practical matter, I don't think that can be denied.

COHEN: Really . . . ? Then I suppose I'm confused about how one experiences truth. It seems to me that truth is . . . a state of being . . . a condition of the world— that being one of accuracy with respect to reality.

JAMES: Give me an example of what you mean.

COHEN: Well . . . look . . . it is without question that Mr. Cleveland is the president of the United States. That is the truth. It exists as a condition of our world. I don't experience Mr. Cleveland as president. He just *is* president.

JAMES: (a bit perplexed) I disagree with your claim that we don't experience him as president . . . but let's not quibble on that point for now. Let me attack the issue another way. (James pauses a moment, thinking) Well . . . let's suppose you overhear a conversation between two Englishmen while visiting London, and it's quite clear from their talk that they are under the impression that Mr. Stevenson is president. Would you not be inclined to politely intervene and correct them?

COHEN: I might.

JAMES: Right. Notice how in this example you're using truth to guide your actions. The truth is that Cleveland is president, and that knowledge compels you to intervene in the Englishmen's conversation.

COHEN: Okay . . . ?

JAMES: But let's change our scenario somewhat. Let's suppose that you had been misinformed about the state of the presidency and were quite convinced that Mr. Stevenson was the president. With this in mind, you overhear the same conversation between the two Englishmen . . .

COHEN: (puzzled) Well . . . yes . . . okay.

JAMES: Under these conditions you would behave differently. You'd remain aloof from the Englishmen and merely think to yourself, "How well it speaks of the English that they keep up so closely with American affairs."

COHEN: . . . Possibly . . . yes. I'm not sure I'm following your point . . .

JAMES: My point is a pragmatic one. You see, whatever it is that we might call truth, when it becomes a practical matter of functioning in the environment, truth is what we use to guide our actions.

COHEN: What we use to guide our actions . . . ?

JAMES: Right. In one case, thinking that Cleveland was president, you intervened in the Englishmen's conversation. In the other, thinking Stevenson was president, you did not. In both cases, your action was guided by what you held to be the truth.

COHEN: So you're reducing truth to merely what is useful for guiding one's actions.

JAMES: Yes. Truth is useful. Whereas untruth is not.

COHEN: Well . . . I guess that is the nub of our disagreement. I don't think truth means "whatever is useful."

JAMES: Why not?

COHEN: Because truth is more than just utility. Truth is . . . well . . . it's something sacred. People live and die for truth.

JAMES: I agree. Truth is important. But why is it important? I believe taking a pragmatic approach helps us better understand exactly what it is about truth that makes it so valuable.

COHEN: A pragmatic approach? What do you mean?

JAMES: Let me explain it this way: You say that reducing truth to utility devalues it. Truth is too important to be thought of this way.

COHEN: Right.

JAMES: But I could ask, what makes something valuable or important? Name for me something that is of great importance or value to you.

COHEN: Well . . . I'd say right now . . . getting my degree . . . getting good grades. Yes. Right now, at this point in my life, I think that is probably of greatest importance.

JAMES: Of course . . . and that is probably what motivated you to seek me out on my way home and question me about this very topic.

COHEN: Yes. I think so.

JAMES: But let's push the issue further. Why are good grades and a Harvard degree so valuable to you? What's the great importance of these things?

COHEN: Well, I think that is fairly obvious.

JAMES: Maybe so, but humor an old man.

COHEN: My degree will open doors to many professional opportunities. My success as a writer or lawyer could depend on it.

JAMES: In other words, a degree from Harvard is important . . . it has great value . . . because it is useful to you in your future professional endeavors—correct?

COHEN: Well . . . yes, I suppose that's true.

JAMES: And by saying the degree is useful . . . that is has great *utility* . . . are we somehow . . . degrading it?

COHEN: No, it doesn't seem so.

JAMES: In fact, couldn't we go so far as to say that if the degree didn't have that utility, it wouldn't be important or valuable?

COHEN: Yes. I see what you're saying. And . . . you would apply this same logic to truth.

JAMES: Right. To better understand something, we focus on its use. We ask, what difference does that thing make in how we live our lives?

COHEN: I see.

JAMES: This is what lies at the heart of a pragmatic approach to philosophical issues. I call it a "fruits not roots" approach to understanding them.

COHEN: Fruits not roots?

JAMES: Yes, rather than worrying so much about the origin of an idea—is it convincingly grounded in unassailable logic or evidence? A question we may never answer to everyone's satisfaction—let's focus on its consequences . . . what grows from the idea, for good or for ill, if we accept or reject it.

COHEN: Okay . . . I can see some benefit to that.

JAMES: So when we debate difficult philosophical issues such as free will or God or . . . *truth* . . . instead of tearing our hair out trying to determine if the idea is logically sound or not, let's focus instead on the *utility* of the idea. Is the idea useful or beneficial? That's what really matters.

COHEN: I see. And so you would claim that the best way to understand truth is pragmatically.

JAMES: Yes. We should apply the standard pragmatic question to truth, just as we would for any other difficult philosophical issue. We should ask, "Grant that an idea or belief is authentic. What concrete difference will that make in anyone's life? How will someone's experience be different if the idea is true compared to if it is false? I like to call this an idea's *cash value*. What is it really worth in terms of how life is lived?

COHEN: And when it comes to truth, you would say that the difference it makes is that if someone believes something to be true, he will use that belief to guide his actions.

JAMES: Yes. That is truth's cash value.

COHEN: All that sounds fine, but we still have the issue of how what I believe to be true corresponds to reality. Or, in other words, how it connects with the actual state of affairs out there in the world.

JAMES: All right. Fair enough. Give me a case in point and we'll work through it.

COHEN: (sighs, pondering a moment) Ahh . . . I've got a good one.

JAMES: Fire away.

COHEN: Let's take our minds back, far back . . . back before there were any permanent cities or civilizations. When humans hunted off the land to survive, and maybe kept a small garden plot.

JAMES: Before Mesopotamia . . . before the Pharaohs of Egypt . . .

COHEN: Yes. Before anyone sailed or studied the skies.

JAMES: Alright . . .

COHEN: Now if you were to ask any of these primitive people the shape of the Earth on which they existed, undoubtedly they would tell you it was a flat surface extending as far off as the eye could see. To these people, the earth was flat—in its entirety, in its totality.

JAMES: Yes . . . probably correct.

COHEN: But what they had in their heads regarding the Earth's shape was inconsistent with the actual state of reality. The truth is that the Earth is a sphere. It is now and it was then. So what they believed was false.

JAMES: (laughing) No, Mr. Cohen, what they believed was true.

COHEN: But that's absurd.

JAMES: (shaking his head) Yes, I can see how this would be frustrating for you. Many of my colleagues have expressed similar frustration. They think I must have taken a hard blow to the head. But I've assured them, and I'll assure you, that I am of sound mind . . . and what our primitive ancestors thought regarding the shape of the Earth . . . believing it to be flat . . . that *was* true . . . as true as the tree you'll walk into if you don't change course, Mr. Cohen.

COHEN: (stopping abruptly) Oh my . . . thank you (sidestepping the tree).

JAMES: Quite alright.

COHEN: (regaining his stride) But . . . that makes no sense. The Earth is not flat. How could their false belief be true?

JAMES: From a pragmatic standpoint, Mr. Cohen, there is an important distinction between *facts* and *truth.*

COHEN: Facts and truth?

JAMES: Yes. Now if you had asked me if it was a *fact* that the Earth was spherical, even back in primitive days when our ancestors were quite convinced of its flatness, then of course I would have to agree. Facts are facts. But our discussion is about truth, not factuality. Truth, pragmatically understood, is about whether that fact, if accepted, makes any difference. Would it?

COHEN: Would it have made any difference?

JAMES: Yes. Would our primitive hunter have changed anything he was doing if you had come along and convinced him that the Earth was spherical and not flat? Would his actions have been guided any differently if he were to adopt this new truth?

COHEN: I suppose not.

JAMES: I agree. His life was lived at eye level and below. It was the ground beneath his feet and the accuracy of his spear that mattered. Neither of these would have been affected by the infinitesimal curvature of the Earth he traversed from his morning trek into the bush to his evening trudge home. As far as his life and experience were concerned, the Earth was flat.

COHEN: I see, so from the point of view of Pragmatism, a fact may exist, but that fact only has . . . shall we say, *truth value*, if it makes a difference in one's life or experience?

JAMES: I'll make a pragmatist of you yet, Mr. Cohen. Now ponder for a moment . . . when in our history does the fact of the Earth's sphericity become consequential in people's lives?

COHEN: I suppose . . . when they start studying the stars. When they viewed eclipses. When they started sailing long distances on the seas.

JAMES: Yes. Yes. When their experiences began informing them that something was amiss with the idea that the Earth was flat. As experience broadened, new facts were uncovered that forced our ancestors to accept new truths. This is what I mean by truth being *made*. Truth is a process.

COHEN: So you're saying that experience is validating or invalidating different truths we have in our heads—is that correct?

JAMES: Yes. If I believe the Earth is flat and then I view an eclipse and see the curved shadow of the Earth sweeping across the face of the moon . . . well . . . I'd better start rethinking my beliefs.

COHEN: Yes. I see . . . but . . . ?

JAMES: What?

COHEN: Might there not be instances where I try to find ways of explaining the experience *without* changing my beliefs?

JAMES: Oh, yes. That's a strategy we often indulge in. We try to *explain away* an experience, especially if it challenges some truth that we hold dear.

COHEN: I could see where this tendency to guard our truths against experience could be the source of conflict among individuals, tribes, and even nations.

JAMES: It is because people sometimes willingly defend their beliefs with lethal force that calling them "truths" is an appropriate label.

COHEN: I'm not sure what you mean.

JAMES: We've just been through a great civil war. Those on one side viewed slavery as an individual right and economic necessity. Those on the other saw it as an abominable crime against human dignity. Both sides could bring facts to bear to support their view. But would tens of thousands have been willing to die if these differing views had been nothing more than opinions? I think not. These were truths by which people ordered their lives and interpreted their experiences. What people held as true about that peculiar institution motivated them to pay the ultimate price.

COHEN: But doesn't this raise another troubling aspect of the pragmatic approach to truth?

JAMES: Another troubling aspect? What are you referring to?

COHEN: The pernicious impact of self-interest.

JAMES: Self-interest . . . ?

COHEN: Suppose I was a southern plantation owner. My wealth . . . my life . . . my family's security . . . all of it rested upon an economic system of enslaved labor. Yet daily I would have experiences demonstrating the inhumanity of that system. But if truth is what is useful, then clearly it was not useful for me to honestly confront these experiences. My strongest motivation would have been to find whatever rationale possible to explain away . . . deny . . . or simply ignore these experiences because of the threat they posed.

JAMES: You raise an important point. The pragmatic view of truth, or of anything for that matter, is firmly grounded in experience. We must take experience seriously. Experience will provide signs or indicators telling us that the truth we hold may be deficient or too narrow.

COHEN: Sign? Indicators? What do you mean?

JAMES: Let's remain with your plantation owner for a moment.

COHEN: Okay . . . ?

JAMES: You would agree, would you not, that no human has only a singular interest guiding their every thought and action.

COHEN: Well . . . I suppose that's true . . . but explain to me what you mean.

JAMES: Our southern plantation owner has concerns apart from mere economic ones. For example, he likes to think of himself as a decent, honest, good Christian man. Couldn't we agree that this is likely to be another important interest of his, along with economic concerns?

COHEN: I suppose. Everyone wants to have a positive self-image. It's reasonable to assume that our plantation owner wants to think of himself as a decent, upstanding man.

JAMES: We could refer to this desire for a positive self-image as an already established "truth" in our plantation owner's mind.

COHEN: An already established truth?

JAMES: Yes . . . no one arrives at their experiences with an empty head. We have a network of background knowledge that we bring to any situation . . . any experience. Preestablished truths about ourselves and our world are part of this background knowledge.

COHEN: Okay . . . that makes sense.

JAMES: Pragmatism would argue that an important test for the usefulness of any new truth is how well it connects to established truths present in our heads.

COHEN: So . . . I think what you're saying is that the inhumanity our plantation owner experiences by being surrounded by enslaved labor does not connect well with the already established truth of his Christian self-image.

JAMES: Correct. Thus, our plantation owner is put into a mentally stressful state. Either he must deny the truth of his decency, or he must . . . as you said earlier . . . ignore or somehow explain away his experiences of inhumanity for which he is responsible.

COHEN: One way of dealing with this stress would be to shield himself from uncomfortable experiences. So he stays away from the fields or the workhouses where he might see mistreatment in the same way that an industrialist avoids the factory floor so that he doesn't witness the deplorable conditions there.

JAMES: Yes. Yes. Whenever a truth is forcing us to restrict our experience so that we can comfortably maintain that truth and not have it challenged, then we must question it. *Experience validates truth.*

COHEN: Or invalidates!

JAMES: Yes.

COHEN: And if we take experience seriously . . . as you advise, then it will inform us about the quality of the truths we hold.

JAMES: Right. A good truth should broaden our experience. It should be a useful tool that allows us to navigate successfully through the widest range of possible experiences.

COHEN: So if we think again about our plantation owner . . . along with avoiding certain parts of his plantation, he may also be inclined to restrict his social interactions as well. He surrounds himself exclusively with other plantation owners and like-minded businessmen.

JAMES: All of whom reinforce his limited perspective on what is true and what is not. But this tendency to seek out only those of our kind, so to speak, is not restricted to just our plantation owner. It's a general human tendency—all of us are guilty of it to one degree or another.

COHEN: And you believe this general human tendency represents another obstacle when it comes to building better truths.

JAMES: Indeed. Another quality that a good, functional truth should have is its ability to withstand refutation. Those whose experiences mirror our own are unlikely to present arguments or ideas that force us to reconsider our truths.

COHEN: But those with very different experiences from us may see the world in a way that we have never thought about before.

JAMES: Yes. What if our plantation owner were to engage in an honest discussion with a committed abolitionist and listen carefully to the arguments he presents? How well would his truth stand against that challenge?

COHEN: As you describe it then, truth is an adaptive property that ideas possess to greater or lesser degrees.

JAMES: Yes, truth is something that happens to an idea. With experience we increasingly recognize that an idea or belief has wider or narrower functional use. The wider the function, the truer the idea.

COHEN: Can we summarize what constitutes an idea with high truth value?

JAMES: Yes. It is an idea that connects well with other deeply held truths that we possess. It is an idea that affords us the widest possible range of experience. It allows us to adaptively steer through a diversity of experiences. High-quality truth is fearless, no experience must be avoided or dismissed for it to retain its integrity. High-quality truth can sustain itself against intellectual challenge. It confronts objections head on without excuses or rationalizations.

COHEN: And it is experience that both validates the quality of our truth or highlights its weaknesses.

JAMES: And once those weaknesses are exposed, it is experience that challenges us to revise and strengthen our truths. This is all part of the truth-making process that, at our discussion's start, you were so skeptical of.

COHEN: Yes, but I think I have a better understanding of it now. However, something still bothers me.

JAMES: Still looking for potentially fatal flaws in a pragmatic approach to truth, are you, Mr. Cohen? That's admirable.

COHEN: Maybe not fatal flaws. But . . . logical inconsistencies.

JAMES: Logical inconsistencies . . . ? What do you mean?

COHEN: I know that you have an aversion to any form of absolutist thinking.

JAMES: True. I think the best way to understand the world is to accept its plurality.

COHEN: Right. I recall you talking about that in lecture. We experience a world of variety . . . of many different forms and systems . . .

JAMES: And this is not illusory. The universe *is* as we experience it—a vast array of diversity.

COHEN: But our discussion of truth makes me question that.

JAMES: In what way?

COHEN: I'm wondering if there might not be evidence for a single, universal concept of truth, or maybe . . . a small set of universal truths.

JAMES: Ahh . . . once again, the never-ending search for universals . . . for absolutes. It seems the human mind has a natural tendency toward simplification. We're never quite satisfied until we reduce complexity down to simplicity. Why should we not try with truth as well?

COHEN: Before you condemn, hear me out.

JAMES: Of course . . . of course. If there's truth in my pragmatic view of truth, then it should be capable of withstanding whatever refutation you can mount.

COHEN: Let's take, for example, a past practice that was regarded as acceptable, maybe even noble in certain cases, which is now judged barbaric.

JAMES: I believe the Spartans can offer us just such an example.

COHEN: Oh . . . what were you thinking of?

JAMES: The Spartans had a practice of casting unwanted children onto the dung heap to die of neglect.

COHEN: Yes. I recall. Any infant that was judged unhealthy or malformed in some way—the parents were expected to dispose of it rather than expend energy and resources on a child that could not live up to Spartan standards of strength and vigor.

JAMES: And this was viewed as more than just a tragic necessity.

COHEN: Oh, yes . . . indeed. It was regarded as a noble duty. It reinforced loyalty to one's tribe over individual self-interest.

JAMES: You might say that "Spartan truth" entailed a belief that love of offspring must be subordinated to love of tribe, even to the extent of sacrificing one's child if he or she did not meet Spartan standards of health and strength.

COHEN: Yes, let's think of it in those terms.

JAMES: So are you asking why we no longer accept the Spartan version of truth on this issue?

COHEN: Yes, but my point is an even larger one.

JAMES: Oh, yes . . . that idea of some convergence on a universal truth.

COHEN: Right . . . now, if you were to go back to the ancient world and ask people to pass judgment on the Spartan practice of disposing unworthy children, wouldn't you agree that most would fall short of an unequivocal condemnation?

JAMES: You're saying that we don't just inquire with Spartans about it, but with Athenians, Corinthians, Thebans, Macedonians, and all the ancient worlders that we could muster.

COHEN: Yes . . . absolutely. We conduct an ancient world survey, if you will.

JAMES: And you believe that few, if any, would condemn the practice.

COHEN: Yes. I think most would find the practice regrettable but necessary; maybe even noble in its valuing of tribe over family.

JAMES: Yes, I could easily envision most saying, "That's the Spartan way. And who am I as a non-Spartan to judge their way of life."

COHEN: Right . . . so we agree that in the ancient world the Spartan truth was largely an acceptable one. How do you believe that truth fares today?

JAMES: Quite poorly, I would hope.

COHEN: And therein lies my point. Today, if you were to engage in that same survey of attitudes regarding Spartan truth, I think you would find almost, if not complete, condemnation. Barbaric and cruel is how most everyone—at least in civilized quarters—would judge the practice.

JAMES: And you see this as evidence of a convergence on a larger, more universal truth?

COHEN: Yes. In the past . . . the Athenians had their truth, the Spartans had theirs, the Thracians yet another. None accepted the other's truth; all accepted that they would be different. But today there appear to be some truths that have broad appeal across different peoples such as dumping one's child on the dung heap is unacceptable.

JAMES: You see this as one instance of a larger movement toward a single universal truth or maybe . . . a small set of universal truths.

COHEN: Potentially . . . yes. You disagree?

JAMES: I can see diverse peoples sharing common truths to the extent that their experiences are similar.

COHEN: So you think it all comes back to experience?

JAMES: Yes. Here's how I see it. People were more isolated from one another in the past. One tribe lived along the seashore and made their living fishing; another in the hills, hunting and tending small gardens; yet a third on the open grasslands, with farms and cattle. Conflict with neighboring tribes was the norm. Athens fought Sparta, the Spartans fought the Persians, Macedon fought with whomever they could find.

COHEN: So this isolation and conflict bred widely varying life experiences for the different tribes.

JAMES: Yes. Not only were their experiences varied, but the differences were emphasized by the need to maintain strong social identities. The Spartan practice of abandoning unworthy children may have been borne of necessity, but it eventually became a prideful source of tribal identity, something that marked them as unique and *tougher* than their rivals.

COHEN: So different tribes tended to emphasize their different experiences and the truths they constructed from them.

JAMES: Yes. Very much so. "That is the Spartan way. Those are Spartan truths. But our ways, our truths are different, for we are not Spartans . . ." That was the attitude, I think.

COHEN: So then you see the convergence of truth resulting from experience growing more . . . overlapping.

JAMES: Yes. There's far less isolation today. We travel more and learn more about the life ways of other people. And with that we are able to find more commonalities among our experiences.

COHEN: There still is much conflict today, however.

JAMES: Indeed, we've just come through a terrible war. But I would argue that there is a great deal more commerce, trade, and communication among people today compared to the past. My brother has spent most of his adult life in Europe rather than America.

COHEN: Yes . . . I see. One might argue that even conflicts have a rather different character today than in the past. Instead of longstanding rivalries, friend and foe often switch roles regularly. We fought alongside our southern brethren against the English, with the French against the English, and before that with the English against the French. Your enemy one day is your partner the next.

JAMES: I would contend that the modern world, in contrast with the ancient world, is one where cooperation among varied tribes is more a priority than conflict. Where this is so, we are motivated to find common ground among our experiences rather than emphasize differences.

COHEN: And it is this increasing common ground in our experiences that you believe is producing a convergence of truth.

JAMES: Yes. Now will this ultimately lead to universal truths or a single universal truth? It remains to be seen. There will always be some differences in our experiences and therefore differences in truth.

COHEN: The important issue then becomes a matter of weight, wouldn't you say?

JAMES: Weight . . . ?

COHEN: Can our common truths outweigh the divergent ones?

JAMES: One can hope that that becomes the case and therefore leads us to greater peaceful cooperation among people and less conflict.

COHEN: Well . . . I see we have arrived at your home. I'm hoping you'll be having another one of those student get-togethers soon. The last one was most enjoyable.

JAMES: As long as you and your peers agree to help clean up next time. The truth is that Alice was rather disappointed with the mess you all left.

COHEN: Give us another chance, Professor James, and we'll give her a different experience.

JAMES: See you in class, Mr. Cohen.

Chapter 7

God and Belief[1]

Topic(s): God, religious experience, and belief

Student: Gertrude Stein

Outline:

Finite versus infinite God
   God as a chess player
   God's nature versus God's volition
   The problem of evil
The origins of morality
   Moral solitude
   Moral claims
   Why morality is hard
The religious experience and the morally strenuous attitude
   The qualities of the mystical experience
   Evidence and belief
   Belief creating its own verification
When do we have the right to believe?

Gertrude Stein

Gertrude Stein was born on February 3, 1874, in what was then called Allegany City (now Pittsburgh). Her childhood was spent in Austria, France, and later Oakland, California. In 1893, she entered Ratcliff College, where she attended William James's lectures on psychology at nearby Harvard. She earned her degree in 1898. In 1902, Stein moved to Europe, eventually settling in Paris, where she

---

[1] This chapter draws upon numerous sources including James's essays, "The dilemma of determinism," "The moral philosopher and the moral life," "The will to believe," The meaning of truth"; James's book *The varieties of religious experience* (especially lectures 14, 15, and 16); and Michael R. Slater, *William James on ethics and faith* (Cambridge University Press, 2009).

and her brother Leo became well-known art collectors, art critics, and writers. Her home became a gathering place for prominent artists and authors of the early twentieth century such as Picasso, Matisse, F. Scott Fitzgerald, and Ernest Hemingway. Her literary style often modeled the "stream of consciousness," advocated by James at Harvard. Stein was also (in)famous for a confusing mix of social/political views raging from pro-immigrant, feminist progressivism to fascist-sympathizing reactionaryism.

It has been a long day of lecturing, meetings, and writing for William James. He's looking forward to a quiet evening with the family at his house on Irving Street. Dark, cloudy skies greet him as he steps out of the hall into the late afternoon air. He studies the sky and then returns to his office to retrieve his umbrella, just in case. Waiting for him at the office door is an impatient student, Gertrude Stein.

STEIN: Oh . . . Professor James, I was hoping I could catch you.

JAMES: Thanks to inclement skies, you did.

James gives her a questioning look. Then he points a deliberate finger at her.

JAMES: Miss . . . Stein. Correct?

STEIN: Yes . . . yes. Gertrude . . . Gertrude Stein.

JAMES: Very good. Glad to know my memory hasn't yet begun to fail.

STEIN: I wonder if I might bother you about some . . . confusions I'm having with your last lecture.

JAMES: Confusions . . . in the plural . . .

STEIN: Well . . . yes. I hope it's not too much, but a few things didn't sit well with me and . . .

JAMES: So I take it this will be more of a discussion rather than a simple one-off question and reply.

STEIN: Umm . . . maybe so.

James retrieves his umbrella and begins heading for the exit door. He motions "you first" as they near the door.

JAMES: Shall we walk . . . ?

STEIN: Oh . . . sure. If you don't mind the company.

JAMES: No . . . no, not at all. I'm used to it. I frequently have companionship on my way home these days.

They pause as James scans the road.

JAMES: Oxford Street or Divinity Avenue?

STEIN: What . . . ?

JAMES: Do you have a preference? I can get home by either Oxford or Divinity. Is one better than another for you?

STEIN: Oh . . . well . . . I think Oxford is the shadier of the two. But with the cloud cover, I suppose that is not so important. Divinity has those grand old homes on the way, very pleasant to stroll by.

JAMES: Divinity it is. Let's hope the rain holds off.

STEIN: Yes, indeed.

JAMES: So Miss Stein . . . you have confusions.

STEIN: Yes. A comment you made the other day . . . it threw me off a bit.

JAMES: And what was the nature of this *off-throwing* comment of mine?

STEIN: That rather casual quip you made about God being a chess player.

JAMES: If I remember correctly, I didn't exactly say that God *was* a chess player. I think I said that we could imagine God being a chess player.

STEIN: Well . . . right. We could image God as a chess player.

JAMES: Right . . . so what's so confusing about that?

STEIN: Well, you went on to claim that God, being . . . *God*, well . . . he would naturally know all the possible moves that you might make . . .

JAMES: . . . Right . . . assuming that you're playing God in a chess match.

STEIN: Yes . . . right, of course. You're playing against God in a chess match . . .

JAMES: (a chuckle) Imagine that for a moment . . . playing God in a chess match. Do you really want to win, I wonder? (they share a quick laugh) But we're getting sidetracked. Right . . . the gist of it was that we could imagine God playing against you or me in a chess match.

STEIN: And God, of course, would know all of the possible moves that you might make, and all of the possible countermoves that he might make and their outcomes.

JAMES: Well . . . he's God after all.

STEIN: But you went on to say that what God doesn't know are the actual moves that you choose to make as the game proceeds.

JAMES: Correct. That's what I said. God knows everything that can be known about chess. And if you play him, there's no move you make that will surprise him, no move you make that he cannot effectively respond to, and there's no question that, in the end, he'll win.

STEIN: But . . . you're also saying that even God does not know exactly how the match will play out—correct? He doesn't know precisely which moves you'll try as the game moves forward.

JAMES: Correct.

STEIN: But doesn't that contradict the traditional Judeo-Christian view of God as being omniscient?

JAMES: It may. I have been accused of being unorthodox in my religious views. If you ascribe to the view that God stands outside of time and knows everything . . . past, present, and future, then yes, my view is unorthodox. If instead, you define omniscience as "knowing everything that *can be known*," then my chess-playing God is omniscient is this regard because the future is not knowable until it becomes the present.

STEIN: Didn't Saint Augustine and other prominent Christian philosophers argue that God does, indeed, stand outside of time.

JAMES: Yes, I think that is the traditional view.

STEIN: So you clearly put yourself at odds with traditional Christian thinking when it comes to the nature of God.

JAMES: Yes, in some regards that is probably true.

STEIN: Why? What do you think is gained by envisioning such a limited God?

JAMES: What do I think is gained . . . ? That's an interesting way to pose the question. Yes . . . I do think there are advantages to positing a finite God as opposed to the traditionally envisioned infinite God.

STEIN: Finite, as opposed to infinite . . . ?

JAMES: Yes, I would argue that the traditional view of God is an infinite one—there are no limits on God's love . . . his power . . . his knowledge . . . etc. But my God is a finite one. Yes . . . yes, God is unquestionably a larger, grander, more powerful, more knowledgeable consciousness than that of man, but I don't think that requires that he be infinite.

STEIN: Why not?

JAMES: Well . . . that certainly is not how we experience God.

STEIN: You think that we experience God as being finite and not infinite?

JAMES: Yes . . . obviously so, I think.

STEIN: What do you mean?

JAMES: Take God's infinite love for example. If it is truly infinite, then why do I experience so much anguish in my life? On a more general scale, why is there so much suffering in the world? When a starving mother cries out to God for mercy on her withering child, where is that infinite love? She would surely confirm that there appear to be limits on divine love.

STEIN: I see. And I suppose we could say the same for God's power, knowledge, justice, and so forth.

JAMES: Yes, most definitely. If God is infinite, then that is surely a philosophical . . . or theological abstraction. (pointing to the skies) It's up there, in the clouds. It's not down here where we experience life.

STEIN: But what you point out is not new to Christian philosophy. Haven't most Christian philosophers . . . again, starting all the way back with Saint Augustine, argued that there's a difference between God's nature and God's volition?

JAMES: Miss Stein, you seem to have a particular liking for the old Bishop of Hippo.

STEIN: Saint Augustine, you mean? I'd say more of a respect or familiarity than liking.

JAMES: Yes, myself as well. Fine fellow, the old Bishop. Sharp mind, sharp wit. And he did try to find a way out when it came to the problem of evil.

STEIN: Problem of evil?

JAMES: Yes . . . as I was describing earlier, if God is all powerful and all loving, then why do we experience evil? As you pointed out, Augustine proposed that God is *by nature* infinite, but he *chooses* to limit himself to allow for human free will, and it is because of this self-limiting that we have evil in the world.

STEIN: Right . . . but you are arguing for something even more radical—correct? That God is *by nature* limited.

JAMES: Yes. I think that is more likely.

STEIN: Why so?

JAMES: Well, as I said before a finite God conforms with our experience, and a finite God avoids other worrisome problems that arise with an infinite God.

STEIN: What do you mean?

JAMES: You've heard me talk in class of Mr. Darwin and his theory of natural selection.

STEIN: Yes, you seem to be quite sympathetic to his ideas.

JAMES: Yes. I think an evolutionary view of nature has much to offer in helping us understand the human mind. But evolution presents some troubles for an infinite God.

STEIN: What sort of troubles?

JAMES: We see that evil was present long before humans arrived. Many predators have evolved highly effective weapons in their pursuit of prey . . . the sharp talons of some birds, the crushing power of the crocodile's jaws, the debilitating poisons of some spiders . . . we may admire these creations as examples of nature's innovativeness, but for their prey they can only be described as diabolical terrors. Couldn't an infinite God find a less gruesome way to feed his creatures?

STEIN: I see what you mean. So you think that evolution forces us to abandon the idea of an infinite God?

JAMES: No . . . that puts it too strongly. It makes it harder . . . not impossible, but harder to hold such a view. Along with this, however, I think the idea of a finite God is a more . . . freeing . . . more morally compelling one.

STEIN: Freeing . . . ? Morally compelling . . . ? How so?

JAMES: My grandfather was a staunch believer in an infinite God. For him, God was a designer . . . a controller of men's destinies. Grandfather had a strong strain of Calvinist thinking in his blood. Everything was preplanned by God and running off as it was meant to be by divine command. For me, that view of the world is too stifling . . . to rigidly confining. There's no room for initiative . . . or freedom . . . or novelty.

STEIN: So you'd rather have a weaker, more limited God running the show, so to speak.

JAMES: Yes . . . yes. Good way to put it. If ultimately God is controlling everything, then do my actions really matter? Why should I bother to set things right . . . or fight for justice, if in the end God is going to square it all up anyway?

STEIN: So you think that an infinite God who ensures the salvation of the world only breeds complacency on the part of believers?

JAMES: No . . . no, again . . . you state it too strongly. I would put it more in terms of tendencies. For many people, an all-powerful God who *ensures* salvation too easily becomes an excuse for complacency. Whereas a limited God who wants the ultimate salvation of the world but needs the active cooperation of humans to achieve it . . . this God serves as a constant source of moral motivation to his believers.

STEIN: How do our actions help God achieve the salvation of the world?

JAMES: With a finite God, the ultimate destiny of the universe is uncertain. We could collapse into bloody chaos . . . a hell of our own making, or we could achieve beatific order. With each act of compassion, forgiveness, unselfishness . . . each *moral* act that we commit, we move the universe closer to that beatific order . . .

STEIN: . . . but with each act of selfishness, cruelty, or violence . . . each immoral act . . . we move the universe toward chaos . . . is that the idea?

JAMES: Yes . . . what if we believed it to be so? What if we truly believed that our actions mattered *that much*. Wouldn't that be a far more morally compelling way to understand the importance of our lives?

STEIN: It sounds as if you think that a finite God is more inspiring than an infinite God.

JAMES: Yes . . . yes. And inspiration is critical to moral action.

STEIN: Inspiration . . . ?

JAMES: Yes . . . the spirit is willing, but the flesh is weak. Most of us want to be decent, moral folks, but the amount of discipline or energy required often causes us to fall short.

STEIN: Moral action requires energy and discipline . . . ? Sounds as if you're saying that we want to help God achieve the salvation of the world, but doing so is frequently just too hard, so we take the easy way out. We make excuses. We look for someone else to do the heavy lifting.

JAMES: Yes. That's a good way to think about it.

STEIN: So why do we end up taking the easy way? Why is morality so difficult?

JAMES: Because morality requires fulfilling the claims that others make upon us.

STEIN: Claims . . . ? What do you mean?

JAMES: Let's start at the beginning . . .

STEIN: Okay . . . ?

JAMES: Imagine a universe with no conscious beings.

STEIN: No conscious beings? You mean a universe with nothing but inert matter floating about?

JAMES: Yes. Exactly.

STEIN: Okay . . . ?

JAMES: Now in this entirely unconscious universe, is morality a relevant issue?

STEIN: Well . . . I'd say . . . no. If all you have is matter spinning about endlessly following nothing but natural law, then no . . . it seems that no moral issues are present.

JAMES: Yes. I agree. Now let's expand our universe just a bit.

STEIN: Okay.

JAMES: Suppose our universe has only one conscious being. An utterly solitary mind among an infinitude of matter . . .

STEIN: A poor lonely soul, I'd say.

JAMES: Indeed. Now do any moral issues arise in this universe?

STEIN: Well . . . again . . . I don't see how.

JAMES: Nor do I. Whatever our lonely mind deems good or ill . . . *is* good or ill, because there is no one else around to challenge that judgment. I think of this circumstance as a *moral solitude*.

STEIN: A moral solitude. I see. So you would say that you need at least two conscious minds inhabiting the universe for morality to emerge.

JAMES: Well, yes . . . that's a necessary condition, but it's not sufficient.

STEIN: Not sufficient? Why not?

JAMES: We could have two conscious minds in our universe, but let's suppose that they are totally unaware of one another. One on *this* side of the universe (James gestures to the left) and the other on *that* side of the universe (gesturing to the right).

STEIN: Thus, each existing in a separate moral solitude.

JAMES: Correct. Or another possibility is that they are aware of one another but completely indifferent to each other. Neither has the least concern for the other's condition.

STEIN: I see. Once again, a moral solitude of sorts, only this time resulting from psychological distance rather than physical distance.

JAMES: Yes . . . a rather good way of putting it.

STEIN: So our universe does not become a *moral* universe until our conscious minds begin to interact or relate to one another.

JAMES: Correct. Part of that interaction being each making claims on the other. "If you do this, I'll do that in return. Help me build my house and I'll share my crops with you. Care for me and I'll care for you." Those sorts of arrangements.

STEIN: Thus, no longer do we have moral solitude but moral communities.

JAMES: Right. And it is here that morality becomes hard.

STEIN: How so?

JAMES: The claim that another makes will require something from us. It will require time, effort, energy, emotional . . . physical . . . material resources.

STEIN: So moral behavior is not free. It has a cost.

JAMES: Yes. And we are always trying to minimize those costs. We're always trying to figure out how to satisfy claims with the least amount of personal effort.

STEIN: Thus, we might be inclined to reject some claims because we see them as too costly.

JAMES: Yes. In fact, I think that would be our natural inclination—wouldn't it? You see, just as others are making claims on us, we are, in turn, making claims on others. And wouldn't there be a natural bias on our part to try to get more from others than what we are willing to give?

STEIN: But if we are always trying to get more than we give, can we call that genuinely moral?

JAMES: Yes. Exactly. That becomes the critical question. Our natural biases toward selfishness and laziness will work against our ability to be genuinely moral.

STEIN: And if this bias is a general one, not just in you and me, but common to all, then how can we hope to build a truly moral community?

JAMES: As I said before: Morality is hard. In the ideal moral community that I envision, the working assumption ought to be that all moral claims are legitimate.

STEIN: Legitimate? You mean that when someone makes a demand on my time, effort, or resources, I should assume that their need is real and that I am obligated to fulfill it.

JAMES: Yes . . . I think that should be the working assumption of all members of the moral community. All members of the community need to be responsible for the well-being of others. That means that we should force ourselves to be more generous, caring, and forgiving than our natural inclinations dictate.

STEIN: Because our natural inclinations will always be toward selfishness and laziness.

JAMES: Yes. Those are the obstacles we must overcome to build a truly moral world.

STEIN: Those obstacles might be insurmountable. For someone who usually preaches pragmatism, have you not fallen into idealism on this issue? Maybe there is no real hope of any sort of altruism in the world. Instead there is only utilitarian morality . . .

JAMES: You mean something like, "I'll be moral so long as it doesn't cost me too much."

STEIN: Yes. Maybe that is the best we could expect.

JAMES: Maybe, but I'm not quite that pessimistic.

STEIN: Oh . . . why not? From where does your optimism arise?

JAMES: Hmm . . . from where does it arise . . . ? I would say from the topic that began this conversation: God.

STEIN: God . . . ? You believe that divine intervention can save us?

JAMES: In a sense, yes . . . but not in the form of miracles or any sort of global, biblical dramatics.

STEIN: Then what? How can God intervene to make us more moral?

JAMES: Maybe through the inspiration arising from religious experiences.

STEIN: Religious experiences? You think that they can elevate our morality.

JAMES: Yes. I think there is some hope of that. If the fundamental problem with moral behavior is mustering up the energy to overcome our selfishness, then the antidote to that is inspiration, and inspiration is what the religious experience provides. It generates the energy necessary for adopting the morally strenuous attitude.

STEIN: Morally strenuous attitude? What does that mean?

JAMES: It means approaching morality with the same attitude as an athlete approaches a competition. One must practice discipline and self-control the way an athlete practices his physical skills. We need to train ourselves so that generosity, compassion, justice, and forgiveness become habits, the same way that an athlete's physical skills become habitual.

STEIN: But most of us are not athletes.

JAMES: Correct. Most of us aren't motivated enough to strengthen our morality the way an athlete strengthens his body. And so, and as you pointed out earlier, we're content with being moral until the cost gets too high.

STEIN: So is this where God comes into play? Is God . . . like a coach or trainer who pushes us to improve our moral skills?

JAMES: To some degree. But I'd put it this way—it appears that humans have the capacity to experience God . . .

STEIN: . . . a religious or mystical experience, such as those claimed by Christian saints or Buddhist monks—is that what you're referring to?

JAMES: Yes. If we study these experiences, we see that they frequently have a morally inspiring quality to them. Christian saints, for example, who claim to have had mystical experiences often show an excess of such attributes as devotion, purity, tenderness, charity, and asceticism. They joyfully endure hardships that you and I would find intolerable.

STEIN: Moral athletes, you might say.

JAMES: Yes. Now sometimes this can go too far. In some saints, devotion went to fanatical extremes that I would not recommend. But overall, the saints provide an example of people who succeeded in living a morally strenuous life.

STEIN: And it was their mystical experience . . . their experience of God, you say, that inspired them to do so.

JAMES: Indeed. I believe it played a critical role.

STEIN: What is a mystical experience like?

JAMES: The experiences can vary. But there appear to be some common features.

STEIN: Such as . . . ?

JAMES: Well . . . there's an ineffability about them . . .

STEIN: Ineffability . . . meaning that can't be described.

JAMES: Correct. The mystic does his best to offer a verbal description, but words can never capture the totality of the experience. It exceeds concepts and language. Yet, despite this, the mystic is convinced that important knowledge was transmitted through the experience.

STEIN: Important knowledge . . . ?

JAMES: Yes, this constitutes the second important feature—mystical experiences are noetic in character. They are a source of knowledge or wisdom. The mystic learns that there is a unity to all things. That he is part of something far more grand and wonderful than what ordinary experience can convey. But even putting it this way is inadequate. Instead the knowledge the mystic has gained must be *lived* because it can't be entirely explained.

STEIN: I see. It is this need to live the wisdom that provides the energy or inspiration for the morally strenuous lifestyle.

JAMES: Yes, I think so.

STEIN: So ineffability and noetic character . . . are there other features?

JAMES: Yes, transience is another. Most mystical experiences are brief, lasting only a half hour or a few minutes.

STEIN: I see.

JAMES: And passivity—the fact that the individual does not control the experience. The person may hasten it through ritual practices, but once in the state, he is overtaken by a greater power.

STEIN: Overtaken by a greater power . . . isn't that a bit of a supposition? Professor James, I can appreciate the mystic's sense of having had a divine encounter, and the positive transformational impact of that encounter. But these are all subjective accounts. Who knows what their source might be? They could be nothing more than fantasy or the result of some brain disease.

JAMES: Possibly. However, if it were a malady then we should expect to see mystics frequently displaying other deleterious symptoms. Instead what we see is that they are often models of virtue.

STEIN: I see . . .

JAMES: I would argue for using a pragmatic approach in assessing the value of mystical experiences.

STEIN: A pragmatic approach . . . ?

JAMES: Yes. It's not the origin of the experience but its consequences that should be primary in determining its value. The mystical experience has largely positive effects . . . it transforms the individual for the better. If it is a form of brain disease, let's hope that more of us become afflicted.

STEIN: Yes, I can see that. But even so . . . I'm compelled to play devil's advocate even more, if it does not try your patience too much.

JAMES: Not at all. The devil is often a source of good conversation. Carry on.

STEIN: Well, I sense that our entire discussion is merely assuming the theist position to be a tenable one. Surely, there are many who would contend that the God hypothesis has been definitively disproved.

JAMES: Oh . . . I'm sure there are those who would claim that. However, I think whether one believes in God or not is far more a matter of temperament than logic or evidence.

STEIN: Temperament?

JAMES: Sure. People's beliefs, including those of scientists and philosophers, are largely based on feeling. They believe whatever it is that makes them feel good. Only after this do they look for evidence or arguments to support that belief. If you are motivated to believe in God, then the various philosophical arguments that have been made on his behalf are likely to impress you. If you're a nonbeliever, then the arguments for materialism and atheism sound unassailable to your ear.

STEIN: Maybe so, but shouldn't all our beliefs have some basis in evidence?

JAMES: Yes. Having a solid evidentiary basis is a desirable quality for any belief—who could contend otherwise? But what constitutes convincing evidence?

STEIN: Can't science determine that for us? If something has been shown to be scientifically credible, then surely it is worthy of belief.

JAMES: And if it has not passed the test of science, then we should withhold belief. Would that be your view?

STEIN: It seems a reasonable rule—no?

JAMES: Reasonable maybe for beliefs that can be scientifically tested. But I would contend that most of the beliefs we use in everyday life, such as whether or not there is a God, don't lend themselves well to scientific methods.

STEIN: Really . . . ?

JAMES: I believe Mozart to be the most important composer in musical history. But I'm sure others would contest this belief. "What about Beethoven or Bach?" they might respond. Now is there a scientific test we can do to settle the issue?

STEIN: Yes . . . I see. A scientific test might be implausible. But there is other evidence we could consult. Number of symphonies written . . . innovativeness . . . popularity . . . influence on other composers...

JAMES: Which one? It seems any measure will likely be contested. Isn't it more likely that those who are already predisposed to favor Mozart will be convinced by evidence in his favor and the same for Bach or Beethoven partisans?

STEIN: I suppose so.

JAMES: And most issues in life fall along these lines, I think. They are questions on which science does not apply well, if at all. Should I marry Alice or stay single? Would it be smarter to remain at Harvard or take the offer at Stanford? Are my thoughts my own or am I just parroting those of my father? The beliefs I form on these issues can be critical to guiding my path in life, but scientific evidence is not going to help much with any of them.

STEIN: Yes . . . I see what you mean. It seems in life that we just gather whatever evidence we can and take our chances.

JAMES: Yes. Our beliefs often entail a certain degree of risk. But what is life without some risk?

STEIN: Nothing ventured, nothing gained as they say.

JAMES: Yes. And sometimes realizing the gain first requires an act of faith. Believing, even in the face of little or no evidence, can become the first step toward achieving.

STEIN: How so?

JAMES: Often for an important goal to become a reality, a belief in it is initially required. Belief sometimes becomes its own verification.

STEIN: Belief becoming its own verification . . . ? What does that mean?

JAMES: Let's take the example of human relationships.

STEIN: Such as . . . forming friendships with others?

JAMES: Yes. But it could just as easily apply to a variety of relationships—romances, business partnerships, employer/employee . . . whatever. The first hurdle we face is often one of likeability or trustworthiness—"Is that person likeable?" "Can I trust him or her?" "Would that person be a good friend?" These are the questions we often ask ourselves.

STEIN: I see. But how does belief create its own verification in these instances?

JAMES: Often the first step toward creating a social connection is to assume . . . or *believe in*, the good intentions of the other.

STEIN: So to determine if someone is trustworthy, I must first be willing to put my trust in them.

JAMES: Exactly. And once they see that another is placing trust in them, they often reciprocate by striving to live up to that expectation.

STEIN: The initial belief thus creates the conditions for its own verification.

JAMES: And without that initial belief, most of us would remain in social isolation. Would any friendships or romances ever get started if we withheld our trust until enough scientific evidence had been gathered to ensure us that the risk was worth taking?

STEIN: Yes . . . yes, Professor James . . . I can see that to function in everyday life we often must form beliefs in advance of convincing evidence. We . . . take risks in life, sometimes . . . it can't be avoided.

JAMES: Yes. And then it becomes a choice between which risk we find more aversive.

STEIN: Which risk . . . ?

JAMES: For some, the risk of missing out on a possible friendship is the one most feared. That person is motivated to extend trust to another. For another person, the risk of being duped . . . of misjudging another's character and being taken advantage of is the greater fear; and so trust is withheld.

STEIN: In either case, a belief is at work, wouldn't you say? The belief that friendship is worth risking exploitation or that it is not.

JAMES: Yes, I agree.

STEIN: Okay, but accepting all this, I still worry we have given our beliefs license to . . . just run amuck.

JAMES: Run amuck . . . how so?

STEIN: Notice that in all the examples we've discussed our beliefs are following from our desires. You desire Mozart over Bach or Beethoven, so you believe that he is the most important composer. You remain at Harvard, despite offers from other schools because, I presume, you like it here. You extend trust to another because you like that person and want him or her to like you.

JAMES: Yes . . . ?

STEIN: Are we now just saying that we have license to believe whatever we desire?

JAMES: No. I think we can identify some guideposts that allow us to say when a belief is reasonable and therefore someone has the . . . shall we say . . . *right* to believe and when they don't.

STEIN: Guideposts . . . such as?

JAMES: First, there's a notion that I refer to as live versus dead options.

STEIN: Live versus dead options?

JAMES: Yes . . . you might think of it as a *prima facia* test for the reasonableness of a belief. A live option means that the person sees a certain belief as plausible, something they might be willing to accept. Whereas a dead option is something they would never consider.

STEIN: For example . . . ?

JAMES: Didn't you mention in class one time that you had an auntie who composed music?

STEIN: (modest laughter) Oh yes, my Auntie Claire. I hope I did not give the wrong impression. Her compositions were nothing more than little pieces she made up while teaching my sister and I piano.

JAMES: Yes . . . well . . . with respect to Auntie Claire . . . and I'm sure her compositions were quite good . . .

STEIN: Delightful little numbers really . . .

JAMES: Yes, of course. But you would agree, wouldn't you, that despite the delightfulness of her compositions, it would not be a live option to believe her to be the most important composer in the history of music . . . in the same category as Mozart, Brahms, or Beethoven.

STEIN: Well . . . as much as I adore Auntie Claire, I'd be inclined to agree with that.

JAMES: I wonder if a good Russian would even consider Mozart, Brahms, or Beethoven given his likely allegiance to Tchaikovsky.

STEIN: Good question.

JAMES: But once a belief is seen as a live option, then it becomes a question of intellectual credibility.

STEIN: Meaning . . . ?

JAMES: Can the belief be judged based on logic or evidence? If logic or evidence convincingly contradicts the belief, then it would be unreasonable to hold it.

STEIN: So as much as I might want to believe that I have become as good a piano player as my Auntie Claire had hoped, the fact that I didn't get accepted into the conservatory stands as pretty convincing evidence that I'm not.

JAMES: If that was the goal she set for you, then yes, I think it would be unreasonable for you to hold that belief.

STEIN: So in your estimation for one to claim the right to believe something, it should be something that is at least plausible on its surface—a live option as you say—and something on which the arguments or the evidence are inconclusive.

JAMES: Yes. Those are the first two important parameters.

STEIN: There are others?

JAMES: Yes, additionally the belief should be one that is forced on us. We must decide one way or another on the issue. For whatever reason, we're not able to withhold judgment until more evidence comes in.

STEIN: Hmm. . . . It would seem that our composer question is not necessarily a forced one. We could defer . . . could we not . . . and merely say that any of those options . . . Mozart, Brahms, Beethoven . . . even Tchaikovsky are all reasonable possibilities.

JAMES: Yes, I agree. But envision a different circumstance. Suppose you had gotten lost on a hike in the woods and had grown dangerously frail and weak. You come upon a trail and must choose whether to take it to the left or to the right. You can muster no convincing evidence to decide the issue one way or the other . . .

STEIN: . . . But I *must choose* because standing still means starving to death in the woods.

JAMES: Right. This is a forced choice because choosing not to believe that either the left or right is your salvation is itself a choice . . . a choice to die rather than be wrong.

STEIN: Yes. I see.

JAMES: Finally, the choice must be momentous, not trivial. The choice must be a consequential one, and therefore the beliefs on which the choice is made are ones to which we are strongly committed. So whether I buy red shoes or brown shoes is trivial. My belief that red is a more desirable color than brown may change tomorrow.

STEIN: But whether one chooses the left or right path is momentous. One's very life may hang in the balance.

JAMES: Correct.

STEIN: I suppose for many, believing or not believing in God is equally momentous.

JAMES: Yes. It could have life-changing effects on how one views the world and one's place in it.

STEIN: It seems to me, Professor James, that you view belief as an integral part of life.

JAMES: Yes. We have no choice but to believe some things in the absence of convincing evidence. Otherwise, we spend a lifetime locked in our rooms, never seeing the sunlight for fear of making an errant judgment.

STEIN: But we can be judicious about what we believe.

JAMES: The person with the right set of sensible beliefs is a wise one, indeed.

STEIN: And belief in God can be part of that set of sensible beliefs.

JAMES: With the correct understanding of God . . . yes, it can be.

STEIN: I believe I see your house just ahead.

JAMES: The evidence seems pretty convincing regarding that belief, Miss Stein.

STEIN: I've enjoyed our discussion, and I look forward to our next class.

JAMES: I as well. Good evening to you.

Epilogue

How Will They Remember Me?

Henry James

Henry James was William James's younger brother, born in New York City, on April 14, 1843. Where William was typically active and exuberant, Henry was more inclined to observant shyness. Henry attended Harvard Law School but quickly found himself more interested in literary pursuits. In 1875, he published his first novel, *Roderick Hudson*. This was followed by over two decades of writing that included such well-known works as *Daisy Miller*, *Washington Square*, *Portrait of a Lady*, *The Wings of a Dove*, *What Maisie Knew*, *The Turn of the Screw*, and *The Golden Bowl*. Henry is regarded as an important transitional figure between literary realism and literary modernism and is thought by many scholars to be among the greatest English-language novelists.

William James awaits the arrival of his brother, Henry, at the landing dock of New York Harbor. Henry, who resides in London, has begun an extended visit back to the States. From the harbor, the two will walk to the train station where they will catch their ride back to Cambridge. Soon enough, William spots Henry making his way down the stairs from the ship to the shore. They embrace and begin their stroll.

WILLIAM: How is London?

HENRY: Gloomy as ever, but busy . . . chatty.

WILLIAM: Alice will be excited to see you.

HENRY: Speaking of Alice, she wrote me a month or so back . . . strange letter . . .

WILLIAM: Oh . . . ?

HENRY: She's convinced that I will be the last to die among us.[1]

---

[1] She was right. Alice James died in 1892, William in 1910, and Henry in 1916.

WILLIAM: Really . . . ? Hmm . . . an interesting conjecture. What do you suppose has gotten her thinking along such morbid lines?

HENRY: I'm not sure, foreboding dreams maybe. In any case, our dear sister was adamant that as the last survivor, I should be prepared to eulogize my departed siblings.

WILLIAM: You're kidding.

HENRY: Not at all. When you and Alice traverse to that undiscovered country, I am to use all my literary skills to memorialize your passings. Furthermore, she insisted that I give it considerable forethought rather than be . . . spontaneous.

WILLIAM: In my case, I prefer spontaneity.

HENRY: No. No. In your case especially, I intend to be fully prepared. In fact, I have already jotted down a few thoughts.

WILLIAM: I hate to disappoint, but I have been exceptionally robust of late. I sense my demise is still some ways off; and, of course, there is always the chance that you could go first.

HENRY: Nonsense. London is gloomy but a far healthier context than Cambridge. Besides . . . Alice is never wrong about these things.

WILLIAM: I see. So, you say you've already begun working on mine.

HENRY: Yes. Yes . . . and I thought it might be fun to run some ideas past you . . . get your thoughts on it while you're still . . . above ground.

Henry reaches into the breast pocket of his coat and unfolds a paper.

WILLIAM: Fun . . . ? We've not laid eyes on one another for over three years and you think it would be fun to discuss my eulogy?

HENRY: You don't want me to misrepresent you to the grieving throngs at your funeral, do you?

WILLIAM: (resigned) Okay . . . so what do you have so far?

HENRY: I thought I'd start with something like this: "Dear friends, you all knew my brother William as a scholar, scientist, and philosopher. He was beloved by all, despite his numerous intellectual inconsistencies . . . "

WILLIAM: Inconsistencies . . . ? You can't go two sentences without criticism?

HENRY: I must be honest . . .

WILLIAM: Name me one philosopher who was wholly consistent in his thinking. That I was willing to reconsider some of my ideas . . . modify them somewhat in response to counter arguments . . . that's no sin. It's a sign of growth. Why not present it in a more positive way?

HENRY: See . . . this is exactly why I wanted to run this by you. I'll say that you were beloved "because of your willingness to admit your flaws and grow from them." How's that sound?

WILLIAM: (sarcastically) Wonderful (musing). My problem was that I wrote so much on so many topics . . . it was inevitable that I would contradict myself here and there.

HENRY: Sure . . . sure. All philosophers with a great body of work have inconsistencies, as you say it's inevitable. It's the . . . broad outlines . . . the general themes and patterns . . . that's what's most important. I need to boil you down to one or two core themes.

WILLIAM: Boil me down . . . ?

HENRY: Yes. Yes. I need to give the heart-sick masses a solid takeaway. So when they leave the graveside they can say, "Ahh . . . yes. That's what old William was all about. That was his essence."

WILLIAM: My essence . . . ?

HENRY: Right. What do you immediately think of when you think of Plato?

WILLIAM: Socrates.

HENRY: No, no. I mean regarding his ideas. Forms. Forms! When you think of Plato, you think of forms. When you think of Kant, you think of innate categories. When you think of Berkeley, you think of ideals. That's what I need for you. When one thinks of William James, what should immediately pop to mind?

The two pause and look at each other momentarily.

WILLIAM: Well . . . I'd say . . . experience. Yes, experience.

HENRY: Right. That's it. *Experience*. It all comes back to experience, doesn't it?

WILLIAM: Yes. Experience, and I'd add . . . pragmatism. Yes. Pragmatism.

HENRY: No, not pragmatism. You and your pals are still arguing over what that means. How about if I call it . . . common sense. Yes. Common sense. That works, I think.

WILLIAM: It's my funeral. Do I get a say in this?

HENRY: Of course. You object to common sense?

WILLIAM: (sigh) No. I suppose I can live with that.

HENRY: Hah! Live with that. Your irony is sharp for a man on death's door.

WILLIAM: Yes, when you . . . boil me down, as you say . . . I don't think you need to stray far from those two ideas. Experience and common sense. Tell my mourning hordes that I believed firmly that all our philosophizing gets needlessly complicated when it becomes unmoored from those things: experience and common sense.

HENRY: Perfect. I'll tell them—"I knew Will as a simple man. He sought to explain human life using experience and common sense."

WILLIAM: There you go. A ten-second eulogy. Attendees will appreciate your brevity.

HENRY: Now, the question becomes: How well did it work?

WILLIAM: What?

HENRY: How well did it work? I'll have to say something about . . . how successful you were or *weren't* in your enterprise. We already know that there were some logical inconsistencies, so I won't belabor that point.

WILLIAM: I appreciate that. Hmm . . . how well did it work? Good question . . . I'd say . . . yes . . . there are several lessons we can draw from this. I think experience and common sense tell us quite a bit about human life.

HENRY: Good. Good. This may be a stirring eulogy yet. Lessons. What do experience and common sense tell us about life?

WILLIAM: They tell us that we are free. Free to change for the better if we're willing to accept the burdens of doing so.

HENRY: That's good. Yes. That's a good one. They'll love it.

WILLIAM: They tell us that the universe is a plurality, not a monism.

HENRY: (obviously disappointed) No . . . no. That will never do. Plurality . . . monism. I'm giving a eulogy, not a Harvard lecture. Whatever does that mean?

WILLIAM: An interconnected diversity of *stuff* . . . that's what we experience. Not a single unified substance. Tell them I hated our incessant drive to reduce everything. Reduction simplifies, but at the cost of exclusion.

HENRY: Reduction simplifies but at the cost of exclusion. That's a good one. I'll have to remember that. What else?

WILLIAM: Experience tells us that we use reason to justify our sentiments, and that *our* supposed objectivity is as questionable as our neighbor's.

HENRY: Why William . . . that's borderline brilliant. I may have been underestimating you all these years.

WILLIAM: A prophet finds honor in all but his own household.

HENRY: What else? I need to fill up at least, ten . . . fifteen . . . minutes.

WILLIAM: Experience tells us that we build truth incrementally just as we build wisdom.

HENRY: . . . Truth and wisdom . . . keep at it, you're on a roll.

WILLIAM: Experience tells us that there is an elegant unseen moral order to the universe and when we attune ourselves to that, we flourish.

HENRY: Yes . . . yes. The unseen moral order. Mentioning that will highlight your mystical side. Appropriate for a funeral, I think.

WILLIAM: Tell them I took God up on his offer.

HENRY: What . . . ? God made you an offer?

They pause their walk again and William gently pushes a finger in Henry's shoulder.

WILLIAM: What if at the beginning of time God said to you, "I'm offering you a chance to be part of a world whose fate is uncertain. If you trust me, yourself, and your companions; and all of you do your level best to be virtuous and brave, then we can redeem this fallen creation. But it's up to us and it won't be easy. Nothing is guaranteed." Would you accept?[2]

HENRY: It's not my eulogy.

WILLIAM: Experience tells us that life is a perilous adventure, and each of us plays a small but crucial role in saving the world from ruin. That's what makes life worth living.

HENRY: That will leave them with a good memory indeed.

THEY STEP ONTO THE TRAIN TO CAMBRIDGE.

---

[2] James presents this scenario on page 139 of *Pragmatism*.

References

Barzun, J. (1983). A Stroll with William James. Chicago: University of Chicago Press.

Feinstein, H. M. (1984). *Becoming William James*. Ithaca, NY: Cornell University Press.

Goodman, R. B. (2012). William James's pluralisms. *International Review of Philosophy, 2*, 155–76.

James, W. (1890). *The principles of psychology*. Henry Holt and Co.

James, W. (1896a). *Is life worth living?* S. Burns Weston.

James, W. (1896b). *The will to believe and other essays in popular philosophy*. Longmans, Green and Co.

James, W. (1899). *Talks to teachers on psychology and to students on some of life's ideals*. Henry Holt.

James, W. (1902). *The varieties of religious experience*. Longmans, Green and Co.

James, W. (1904). Does consciousness exist? *Journal of Philosophy, Psychology, and Scientific Methods, 1*, 477–91.

James, W. (1905a). The place of affectional facts in a world of pure experience. *Journal of Philosophy, Psychology, and Scientific Methods, 2*, 281–87.

James, W. (1905b). The thing and its relations. *Journal of Philosophy, 2*, 29–41.

James, W. (1907). *Pragmatism: A new name for some old ways of thinking*. Longmans, Green and Co.

James, W. (1908). The pragmatist account of truth and its misunderstanders. *Philosophical Review, 17*, 1–17.

James, W. (1909). *A pluralistic universe*. Longmans, Green and Co.

James, W. (1975). *The meaning of truth*. Fredson Bowers (Ed.). Cambridge, MA: Harvard University Press.

Krueger, J. W. (2006). The varieties of pure experience: William James and Kitaro Nishida on consciousness and embodiment. *William James Studies, 1*. http://www.jstor.org/stable/26203679.

Myers, G. E. (1986). *William James: His life and thought*. New Haven, CT: Yale University Press.

Slater, M. R. (2009). *William James on ethics and faith*. Cambridge: Cambridge University Press.

Note: Unless published as an article or book, all of James's essays cited in this book can be found in James, W. (1896b). *The will to believe and other essays in popular philosophy*.

Index

About the Author

Matt J. Rossano is a retired professor of psychology. For over thirty years, he taught at Southeastern Louisiana University in Hammond, Louisiana, after receiving his PhD from the University of California at Riverside in 1991. He is an evolutionary psychologist who has authored or coauthored scores of scholarly papers, book chapters, commentaries, and reviews. His work has appeared in highly respected scholarly journals such as *Psychological Bulletin, Cognition, Current Anthropology, PaleoAnthropology,* and *Cambridge Archeological Journal,* as well as more popular outlets such as *Men's Health, New Scientist, The Huffington Post, Smithsonian Magazine,* and *Psychology Today.* He is the author of several previous books including *Supernatural Selection: How Religion Evolved* (2010); *Mortal Rituals: What the Story of the Andes' Survivors Tells Us About Human Evolution* (2013); and *Ritual in Human Evolution and Religion: Psychological and Ritual Resources* (2020). He is also coeditor (and chapter author) of two recent volumes on psychology and cognitive archaeology.